ME AND MY SHADOW

A Memoir of

a Bipolar Journey,

Embracing the Shadow

Anna Bowditch

Copyright © 2025 by Anna E Bowditch.

Book cover & acknowledgement illustrations by Roseanna Courtney.

The right of Anna E Bowditch to be identified as the author of this work has been asserted in accordance with the Copyright, Design & Patents Act 1988.

All rights reserved. This book or any portion thereof may not be reproduced, distributed, or transmitted in any form or by any means. This includes photocopying, recording, or other electronic or mechanical methods without the author's prior written permission, except for the use of brief quotations in a book review or article.

ISBN: 9798308304203

For my Mum, Jesame, who has been my invaluable 'sidecar' steering me through my bipolar journey. She is a true role model of resilience and inspires me to be the best version of my newfound self.

In memory of my dear Dad, Peter, and other early childhood bereavements.

"There's so much grey to every story - nothing is so black and white."

-Lisa Ling.[1]

---

[1] Quotation by Lisa Ling. Taken from BrainyQuote.com. Website: https://www.brainyquote/quotes/lisa_ling. Retrieved April 14, 2019.

Contents

1. Dual Carriageway Drive
2. D-Day
3. Another World
4. What is in a Label?
5. Surviving the Setbacks
6. Kissing a Few Frogs
7. Being 'Grey'
8. Everybody Needs a 'Sidecar'
9. Mum's the Word
10. Nurses Get Sick Too
11. Like an AAA Battery: Acceptance
12. Like an AAA Battery: Adaptation
13. Like an AAA Battery: Accomplishment
14. Roadworthy

Acknowledgements

Disclaimer

Author Biography

Preface

The mental health drive I found myself on was a consequence of a bipolar diagnosis. I have felt compelled to write my story, allowing you the reader, to walk in my footsteps and comprehend what an unexpected mental health diagnosis can entail. My documented journey can happen to anyone, and it can strike unannounced. My story sets out to provide insight and hope, also addressing the loneliness that can be felt from such a diagnosis. This book not only reaches out to fellow bipolar sufferers but also to parents, significant others and healthcare professionals across the board.

I hope that you can relate to my very own ten commandments and realise that:

1) You will get there, wherever there is.
2) There is life beyond the depressive lows, manic highs, psychosis and crises.
3) Life is only as pressurised as you make it.
4) Just be good enough, there is no such thing as perfection.

5) Life is one big education.
6) Pace and plan, this is my motto for life!
7) Everybody is on their own journey, live your life at your own pace.
8) There is always an opportunity to come back from the brightest and darkest of places.
9) Don't let a diagnosis be an obstacle. You may just have to take a road diversion because of it.
10) Mental health is everybody's business.

Concerning healthcare professionals, 'Me and My Shadow' endeavours to contribute to their knowledge base about this diagnosis in a less conventional way. The tone of this type of bipolar education is a little different from learning about it from a lecturer or textbook. It shares personal lived experiences in abundance and is simply my take on my mental health detour.

As well as helping others, writing has been a form of therapy. I have found it cathartic to bash the laptop keys and release my thoughts. Writing is another tool in my self-care toolkit. Interestingly, I have written in times of mania, depression, in crisis and during hospitalisation. Putting pen to paper has been fragmented, with my flow reflecting the mood episodes I experienced. The later chapters have been drafted when my mental health has been more consistently balanced. Writing even filled the void the Coronavirus lockdown brought.

I hear the question: "What is the significance of the title Me and My Shadow?" It has no relationship to the famous song whatsoever. This poignant name came to me during my first introduction to mental health services. While in the secure unit, I had a 'shadow' of a one-to-one nurse at all times. It later occurred to me that the lows, highs, psychosis and the diagnosis of bipolar have all collectively been shadows in the background of my life throughout this journey.

The use of the term 'shadow' is not too dissimilar to how Winston Churchill described his depression using the 'black dog' analogy. On a more positive note, as I have moved into the recovery stage of my mental health drive, I have been keen for this shadow to remain, but not in the extreme tones of black and white that it used to present.

My bipolar journey has not been straightforward. As my back cover reflects, my shadow has passed through and merged with shades of black, grey and white. In times of mania, it has been the brightest of whites. In contrast, when in deep depression it has become the darkest of blacks. With time, I have learnt to accept and respect my newfound grey shadow which bipolar and my neurodivergent ways have shaped.

Writing has been my private outlet, and it is now becoming public. In doing so, I hope my memoir will aid family, friends, colleagues and acquaintances in making sense of the car crashes that have gone before. I am living proof that recovery takes time and you can live a good life with a mental health past. It is possible to learn to live with your shadow and get respite from the highs and lows.

Deciding to write has provided a platform, allowing me to grow personally, transform and heal. Putting it in print has provided an opportunity for me to shelve the more traumatic elements of the diagnosis, permitting me to move on.

Please accept that my memory has not always been the sharpest. My mental health journey has not been a weekend jaunt, it has felt more like a pilgrimage. If you are a 'Guern', you can comprehend that my journey has had more twists and turns than the Val Des Terres! Days, weeks and years have merged. Therefore, my accounts may be a little distorted, with some inaccuracies likely.

More colour could have been added to my memoir. I have faced some restrictions due to living within such a small community and having only one local mental health facility. Some fellow patients that I have crossed paths with and memorable situations that I have been part of have been omitted, respecting identities.

It was in my thirty-fifth year that my scribblings finally came together. This book describes how I have hypothetically been 'taken off the roads.' I am continually learning to drive that brain of mine again. During the years of journaling, I have deliberated about whether I should write about my story publicly.

It has taken time to find the confidence to speak openly about my Bowditch bipolar brain. Being a nursing professional is one of the main reasons why I was hesitant to voice my struggles publicly.[2] However, to a large degree, it is a transparent and candour account for you to get a true sense

---

[2] In 2021, I sought advice regarding sharing my bipolar story, and via a telephone conversation, I was reassured by my governing body, The Nursing and Midwifery Council, (NMC).

of how turbulent my unexpected mental health road trip has been. I have worn my heart on my sleeve.

The optimistic later chapters of the book are the ones to hold on to. I have finally got my mental health in good order, making a healthy comeback from my secure unit days. As I have learnt, some of the greatest of life's lessons can be found when you are in the darkest of places. Sadly, several fellow mental health sufferers that I have met along the way, are no longer here to tell their stories. I am therefore proud, seeing it as an honour to be able to tell mine.

Making mental health less of a taboo and turning my initial feelings of shame upside down has been my focus. I was keen for this open discourse about my mental health journey to be stigma-busting. A pseudonym was considered when writing this book. Still, I decided that being anonymous would have felt wrong, considering how important I feel it is to speak openly.

A mental health nurse who cared for me, once said: "Don't be ashamed of your story, it will most certainly inspire others when the time is right." Alongside the hope that my story will inspire others, the creation of this book is a personal achievement in itself.

My Victoria Wood style wit is not meant to make a mockery of mental health. The comical edge has helped me to make light of the dark tunnel I have been driving through. Laughter is the best medicine, as they say! While on the subject of iconic people, like Forrest Gump, running has been my saving grace. As he famously said in the film: "Life is like a box of chocolates, you don't know what you're going to get."

I never envisaged a psychiatric diagnosis being assigned to me, let alone section papers! To be truthful, I doubt anyone would purposefully choose a mental health chocolate out of that box. Life is a lottery and we individually have to get on with what we have been uncontrollably dealt.

Putting my nursing hat on, I came to realise that the human body is such a complex structure. Like any other organ, the human brain can have hiccups too. I believe my head when poorly, should be viewed as equally as any other part of the body. However, I am saddened to say, that it is not largely viewed in this way.

We must remember that mental health does not discriminate. It can affect people of all ages, genders, ethnicities and socio-economic backgrounds.

Me and My Shadow

Bipolar can cause a battlefield scene. Active attempts have been made to put the gunfire to rest. You will travel with me to both ends of the bipolar spectrum. Despite the spaghetti junction crossing, you will come out having had a full vehicle 'MOT!'

Before you begin reading my story, I ask you to put the diagnosis of bipolar affective disorder to one side. As you turn this page, I flashback to the Anna who was naïve and had no idea that her life was going to implode and catapult her into a mental health nightmare.

Before getting seated and buckled up, a safety briefing is necessary:

1) The first few chapters are truthful, sincere and dark.
2) As you read on, the road trip will pass through a tunnel with the hope of light at the end, leading to a more optimistic read.

I hope you can relate to my scribblings...

Anna Bowditch

Dual Carriageway Drive

Looking back, things weren't right when I was seventeen. I was a placid teenager and did not give Mum any grief. My struggles started in sixth form. My depressive presentation was initially put down to the delayed grief of my late triplet sister, father, uncle and exam pressure.

Initially, antidepressants were prescribed by a general practitioner, (GP), that I never usually saw. As I later learnt, it is not recommended to prescribe antidepressants to anyone with my diagnosis without a mood stabiliser. It can promote mood switching like rapid cycling between mood states of highs and lows. However, I did not have a known diagnosis at this time. This presentation was only the beginning. Consequently, we later learnt that the medication was a contributory factor in fuelling a manic style of living, which soon followed.

By the age of twenty-three, my chaotic life had ramped up. For a period, my life was like driving full throttle on a 'dual carriageway.' A collision with impact was inevitable as there were two journeys simultaneously happening in just one brain:

1) 'Anna drove car one'. I was trying to carry out the normal activities of life: cooking, cleaning, shopping, eating, sleeping, being a nurse, a daughter and a friend to many. I was also travelling and volunteering abroad.

2) 'Annie drove car two' more destructively. Real life was merged with delusional situations. In these fictitious scenarios which I thought were real, meetings took place with social workers, family liaison officers, police, and bank managers. Unbeknown to me at the time, this was in fact psychosis.

Living a lie is how I can best describe my drive on the 'dual carriageway.' I believed everything, and consequently lived and breathed what has now been diagnosed as a psychotic episode. The mental health charity, 'MIND', explains that a psychotic person perceives and interprets reality very differently from the general public.[3] As I sadly

---

[3] Accessed mind.org.uk on 05/05/24, went onto 'Information and Support', then 'A-Z Mental Health' then 'Psychosis.'

experienced, it is typically characterised by radical changes in personality, impaired functioning and a distorted sense of reality. Delusions were the focal point. Fitting in with this explanation, the 'two cars' intermittently crossed paths. I was trying to live whatever a normal life was, by remaining the driver of car one but kept being overtaken by car two. The vivid and what I believed to be a real psychotic situation engulfed my life. This psychosis was the beginning of that darkening shadow.

This psychotic situation did not occur in reality. Those who know my dear Mum, know that our relationship before this time was the envy of many friends. An argument was as rare as how frequently a fan belt needs changing on a car. The realisation that my entire psychosis centred on her has been a hard concept to accept for both of us. I have later been reassured that psychosis can often feature the people you love the most.

In my mind, Mum had fraudulently stolen ten thousand pounds from my bank account, causing them to be frozen. Voices of bank managers kept demanding meetings with me. I believed my brothers were involved in this conspiracy too.

With all this going on in my bumper car brain, I began to struggle to maintain normal daily life activities. This situation hijacked the 'car that Anna was driving.' As the psychosis went on, more hours of each day were consumed by it. Not surprisingly, I could not stand being at home, it was like a war zone. I resented Mum. As a result, I vividly remember taking up the skill of sofa surfing. Erratic living is the best way to explain my behaviour leading up to and during this psychotic episode:

- I functioned on a few hours sleep a night.
- I filled every second of my time.
- I had a plethora of plans and aspirations which never came to fruition.
- As my manic and psychotic state escalated further, my real car got bashed about. My own car had frequent visits to my local garage. My insurance company knew my insurance number off by heart!
- I had reduced awareness of risk.

Not only did I live through the psychosis, but my family, close friends, nursing friends and work colleagues all endured, what I can safely say, was the scariest period of my life. They did not know it was psychosis at the time, but they all knew things weren't right. When anyone goes through a hard time in life, they commonly turn to a friend for support. In my head, the psychosis was real and I needed someone to turn to. A close work colleague and friend went through so much with me pre-diagnosis, helping me to conquer the 'dual carriageway' journey. She believed my psychotic situation as it was so convincing. Alarm bells rang rather late for her.

Eventually, things didn't add up and that is when my mental health was questioned. We both now have many a laugh when reminiscing. She was in fact at the end of the 'dual carriageway', witnessing the much-needed crash of both cars.

Living and breathing the psychosis for so long caused me to feel imprisoned. I cannot begin to comprehend how my psychosis made Mum feel when she learned that she was at the root of it all. My 'dual carriageway drive' was eventually explained to her by healthcare professionals, allowing her questions to be answered.

It became apparent, that there were a lot more threads to my psychosis when meeting up with friends who had previously lived and breathed it with me. It is amazing what they have recalled, but for me, it is all still a blur. I have found it incredibly tough to make sense of it all. It appears that I have blocked out a considerable amount of the details of this chaotic period of my life. During subsequent hospitalisations, I spent hours writing about the psychosis, breaking it down to find meaning to it all, but with little success.

D-Day

With life events, many people speak of this adage: "It had to get that bad to get better." This was the case with my overpowering psychotic shadow and I. Suicidal thoughts made an appearance before the inevitable car crash. They darkened that shadow even more. This was an extreme change in thoughts from the manic lifestyle and outlook I had adopted as my norm. It was difficult to comprehend how life was worth living when every day mirrored a bumper car fairground ride. At twenty-three, I found myself wishing my life away.

I was a closed book by this time, becoming introverted. My bubbly character and spark had long gone. An hour didn't go by without me questioning my existence and future. Even now, I am finding it difficult to write about the concept of suicide. Anyone who knows me would know that when mentally well, the act of suicide contradicts my core beliefs and values as a person, and more importantly, as a nursing professional. With this in mind, this chapter speaks volumes and indicates how unwell I had become. No one should have an opinion on suicide until the 'shoe is on the other foot.' Amid my mental health journey, Mum was on the receiving end of this comment: "I did not think Anna was the type to attempt suicide?" Mum's response was: "Who is the type?" Quite frankly, I believe no one is immune to this potential act.

Thursday 25th April 2013 came; this date is etched in my brain. The psychosis on this day gave me no relief and became a thick fog, like we so often experience in Guernsey. I no longer felt intact. Having a duty of care to my patients and myself, I realised I could no longer nurse.

On this Thursday, I attempted to take my life. As I was driving to the cliffs, my car broke down in rush hour traffic. My mind was in a spin. I never responded to the orange fuel warning light that had been threatening for some time. My static car prevented the flow of traffic. The toots and stressed drivers added to my frustration. I phoned a friend. She came to my rescue.

Instantly, she saw the turmoil I was in and called on the rest of a supportive group of friends. My car keys were confiscated and it was clear I was mentally and physically stuck. The day ended with me being whisked away in an ambulance with a police car following behind. After seeing the duty GP, and later the duty psychiatrist, my mental health ordeal was unravelling, but only just beginning.

At long last, I was given the get-out clause to leave the 'dual carriageway' and never get into the 'two cars that Anna and Annie were driving' again. This was classified as setback one. Both of me had been pulled over to the hard shoulder. I was transferred to our local psychiatric hospital for much-needed restoration.

Another World

Morning had broken on my local psychiatric ward. I felt like a watch that had stopped. My car had well and truly conked out. I found myself in a personal lockdown.

- Was this all happening to me?
- Who had I become?

Despite many bereavements at such a young age, my childhood was extremely happy and wholesome. I was head or deputy head girl at each school I attended and gained top commendable GCSE, A Level grades and a first-class honours degree in nursing. Lots of dancing and music exams were achieved. My vision was clear as to where my nursing career was going. Volunteer opportunities and projects in poverty-stricken countries were undertaken; some solo and others with friends.

Following the memorable day of Thursday 25th April 2013, it was a rude awakening to find myself on suicide watch. With a click of a finger, I went from being functional and free, to dysfunctional. It was a startling realisation. My world had been turned upside down. It was not what I wanted or planned. A whole new realm of nursing and illness was exposed to me, with me being on the other side of the fence. My shadow had become jet black.

Being deemed high-risk, I had a nurse watching my every move. In mental health speak, this was called 'level three observations.' Movement was minimal. Like a tortoise, I went into hibernation. When I surfaced occasionally, I was faced with a handful of patients I had previously nursed myself. The joys of living on a close-knit island! This made things more awkward.

After three days, due to risk and confidentiality, it was decided that I was to be flown off island, leaving the local ward and my life as I knew it.

It was a Monday morning, by no means a manic Monday! This was the first time that I had wished for fog, but it was a beautiful clear sky day. Two nurses were required to facilitate my transfer. This was a reality check. At eighteen, I had flown solo to volunteer abroad and now I couldn't be deemed safe to go to London alone. When boarding the aircraft, a last-minute runway escape was attempted, but my two nurse chaperones were quick off the mark. The taxi ride from the airport to the London hospital was relentless. I felt like a car waiting to go on the scrap heap.

We approached the grounds of a mental health hospital in the Kensington Chelsea area, and all I could see were big stone buildings and bleak surroundings. My life felt like it couldn't get any worse, but suddenly it had. I felt terrified and strangely numb.

The psychiatric intensive care unit, (PICU), was a twelve-bed female unit, covering ages from eighteen to sixty-five. When entering the locked ward, I was overwhelmed. Watching the two Guernsey nurses reluctantly leave for their return flight home, reminded me of being a child starting school, being dropped off at the school gates.

Soon after my arrival, I was taken into a side room. Here, I was met by a social worker, an independent GP, a psychiatrist and her associate. Structured questions were asked, assessing me against the criteria for detainment.

It went without question that their care decision was to section me. I was put under Section 2 of the Mental Health Act 1983, for twenty-eight days. My shadow was becoming darker by the day. Being sectioned was not on my bucket list! The charity 'MIND', explains the meaning behind the term 'sectioned' simply.[4] They outline that a section can be used to maintain the safety of a patient, enabling assessments and medical treatment to be undertaken. Upon reflection, I now agree that the professional decision of the team at this hospital was one hundred per cent in my best interest. My safety for my life was at huge risk, but I was sadly too unwell to care, rationalise or acknowledge this at that given time.

Initially, I simply could not work out how this mental health secure unit would help me to turn around my overpowering suicidal thoughts. Moreover, I could not comprehend that I was in there. It was hard not to believe that such a barbaric secure unit would be counterproductive to my general wellbeing. I was failing to make sense of it all. A week before, I was still living on a 'battlefield', being at war with 'Anna and Annie.' I ate the psychosis for breakfast, lunch and dinner. Then, it all came to a head. James Bond movies aren't as action-packed in such a short space of time as this:

- Scene One: I woke up on our local psychiatric ward.

---

[4] Accessed mind.org.uk on 13/02/24, went onto 'Information and Support', then 'Legal Rights' then 'Sectioning.'

- Scene Two: I was put on a fighter plane to London.
- Scene Three: I was placed on the front line in a secure unit.
- Scene Four: I lost the battle and was sectioned.

The whole concept of mental health nursing and illness was unknown territory. It felt like I was trespassing. You can't ever settle into a secure unit fully. It took me a good week to accept that I had to stay and make the best of a terrible situation. Until it was taken away from me, being locked in a unit made me realise that I had previously taken for granted the fundamental human right of freedom. I was no longer able to go about my day as I wished.

Being materialistic was something I never considered myself to be. The majority of the contents of my suitcase were confiscated. A glass perfume bottle, drawstring laundry bag, scarves and shoelaces were among the items taken from my reach.

The sudden removal of all these things contributed to making me feel dehumanised. I felt like I was going through airport security, but wished I was going to a nicer destination! The security protocols were carried out primarily for my safety. Regardless, this just helped me to feel more like a criminal as this Monday wore on. Again, I went from being a fully functioning self-caring twenty-three-year-old to not being allowed to carry out basic daily tasks independently.

My sleeping environment was another story. Luckily, I had no trouble sleeping due to the type and amount of medication I was on. My nurse shadow sat in a chair next to my bed for the duration of each night of the twenty-eight days, observing my actions.

With no curtains at the windows and just a sheet to cover me, this sat miles away from my cosy room at home in Guernsey which was full of ambience. The minute I pulled the sheet up closer to my neck in an attempt to try to snuggle, my shadow would pull it down in a brusque way. This basic environment and atmosphere for sleep was a constant reminder of what my life had come to.

Meal times were another matter. We all had to line up, including my one-to-one nurse shadow. Plastic cutlery would be counted out. Consuming the meal was also eventful, as the mood in the dining hall was often fractious. However, we could not get distracted by mealtime mayhem, having to remember to return plastic cutlery so they could be accounted for. This was another routine procedure that caused a tear in my eye: "Bowditch returned spoon, fork, knife", a kitchen lady would state, ticking me off her clipboard.

Unsurprisingly, my appetite was poor in the first week. Due to the commencement of antipsychotic medication, it soon increased and so did my waistline. I ballooned from a size fourteen to a twenty-two in a month, turning into a sloth overnight. Food also became the only focal point of each day. Mum flew over when she was given the green light. She came for the weekend but ended up staying with my eldest brother for the entire duration of my admission, being too distressed to leave.

For mealtimes, we gave Michael Palin a run for his money and 'ate around the world in twenty-eight days', having takeaways most nights from different countries. Although not the healthiest way of eating, this was the only option for us to be able to eat together. It gave us the chance to choose healthier options compared to the food that was being offered on the unit.

Having run at such a fast pace before and during my

psychosis, it felt uneasy and uncomfortable being brought back down to earth with such a bump. A communal sitting area encouraged me to integrate with other patients. This, however, caused me great distress, finding it challenging to see how severe mental health can affect other people.

Bipolar, schizophrenia, schizoaffective disorder and psychotic behaviours were all conditions that fellow patients presented with on the unit. A fellow patient experiencing a phantom pregnancy puzzled me. I was quite confused when she went into 'labour' constantly throughout my twenty-eight-day stretch, producing no baby at the end of it!

Throughout my hospitalisation, I put great effort into trying to remove my invisible nursing hat, but often found myself subconsciously seeing everything through the eyes of a nurse, rather than a fellow patient.

There were attempts to stimulate us. Due to the complexity and unpredictability of all of our mental health conditions, the logistics of getting us all to engage in a therapeutic timetable proved difficult. Art therapy consisted of me having to paint what was in my head; I coloured the entire page black! Hitting a drum randomly shaped the music therapy sessions. Lastly, an occupational therapy assistant,

Me and My Shadow

(OTA), tried to plan a group bingo session. It transpired to be bingo for one. Even my nurse shadow declined to be my competition! After her daily two-hour commute, Mum walked in to see me playing bingo alone, to win a bottle of shampoo that I was always going to win. Priceless! We both chuckle about this to this day.

As well as being a bingo champion, I turned my hand to 'changing the guard at Buckingham Palace.' We were allowed to make two telephone calls a day. Those who have seen me on the telephone, would vouch that I cannot keep still. I put my hypothetical 'black busby hat' on and paced up and down as best I could, given the confines of the payphone cubicle. A pedometer would have clocked up some miles! I almost hypnotised my nurse shadow as he or she watched me through the glass. Being prevented from having outdoor time in the unit's enclosed garden, due to being a non-smoker, was incomprehensible. Mum, with great persuasion, successfully changed this rule for non-smokers, reemphasising the benefits that fresh air and natural light have on general wellbeing.

Even though my accounts of how I perceived the secure unit have had a comical spin, the enormity of this admission was huge. The seriousness was by no means lost. I was desperate for sense to be made of my presentation, realising that it was time for healthcare professionals to get in the driver's seat.

Once a week, Mum and I had to attend a ward round. This type of patient review differed greatly from general nursing. As opposed to daily bedside ward rounds, in this field, reviews were a weekly occurrence. All members of the multidisciplinary team, (MDT), attend. The prominent sound of fingers hitting keys came from the corner of the room, where the associate psychiatrist would be documenting all ward round correspondence. Daunting, is how I would describe this circle time, feeling like I was on Alan Sugar's 'The Apprentice', waiting to be fired.

In my initial week on the unit, the first ward round answered burning questions. In this review, we were informed that the 'dual carriageway drive' that I spoke about in chapter one, was typical psychosis. It was such a relief for my darkened psychotic shadow to have finally been explained. This relief got bigger. My psychiatrist went on to tell us that she felt the psychosis was a result of prolonged untreated mania. Behind the scenes, my psychiatrist had been assessing my history, focusing particularly on my childhood years. She looked further into the possible reasons that could have been responsible for the mania, psychosis and extreme up and down mood patterns. This is when I felt like a baked bean tin, having a Heinz label fitted around it. Bipolar affective disorder (initially type I), was my given label. We were impressed by the psychiatrist I was fortunate to be under. She gave us direction.

Why? This was a question I often asked. Although exact causes are still being looked into globally, healthcare professionals explained the most likely causes that related to me:

> ***Traumatic events:*** I was exposed to many bereavements during my significant early developmental years. At the age of ten months, I lost my triplet sister, Rhia, to meningitis and a congenital heart condition. At the age of five, I lost my dear Dad, Peter, to stomach and metastatic brain cancer. At the age of fourteen, I lost my Uncle Keith, who had become my father figure, to oesophagus cancer. Lastly, at the age of fifteen, I lost my nan, Winifred, due to natural causes.

Genetic factors: The fact that my dear Dad had the diagnosis of manic depression, the old-fashioned term for bipolar, holds a degree of significance. He actively received the invasive treatment of electroconvulsive therapy, (ECT). Genetics is an active area of research, with it being said that there is a strong chance it can be inherited.

Extreme stress: In addition to the stress caused by the documented traumatic events, pressure experienced during exam times at school, degree education and nursing employment, have also contributed to my general wellbeing.

Chemical imbalances: There is some evidence to suggest bipolar can be associated with chemical imbalances in the brain of noradrenaline, serotonin and dopamine.

It is obvious that many adverse childhood experiences, (ACEs), were experienced and manifested in my developmental years. ACEs are described as traumatic events that occur in childhood, from ages nought to seventeen. Experiencing ACEs can produce toxic stress. Our bodies and minds can respond to such toxicity build-up by displaying wear and tear. Toxic stress is impactful on life, which can be displayed in physical and mental illness.[5] Similar to the toll such stress would cause to the mind and body, a car driven for a length of time in the wrong gear would cause harm to the gearbox. With everyone in life, life's stressors inevitably affect our mental health in one way or another.

Becoming educated about ACEs came in the latter stages of my recovery. As part of taking up the lived experience role of 'expert by experience', explained in chapter thirteen, I was involved with trauma-informed care implementation and work around ACEs.

I have seen for myself how important it is for a care team to have a complete picture of your life, both past and present. Rather than asking the question: "What's wrong with you?", the question: "What has happened to you?"

---

[5] Accessed https://developingchild.harvard.edu on 28/04/24, Center on the Developing Child Harvard University, this provided a PDF factsheet on 'What Are ACEs?'

immediately prompts a more holistic assessment. If this stance had been taken with me, then I may not have been given antidepressants so easily when I was seventeen. Also, perhaps other incorrect labels may not have featured throughout my journey.

Although my time in this unit was traumatising and initially negatively viewed, I came to realise it was necessary. The secure unit kept me safe and provided me and my family with a working diagnosis, which was a huge starting point. I had been seven years undiagnosed from when symptoms first reared their head.

These undiagnosed years almost ended in suicide. Although we knew we would have to expect a few more bumps in the road until an individualised treatment plan was figured out, we left the unit with the understanding that I could and would live a good life with bipolar. It was explained that this would take some time to establish, which indeed it did. Keep reading…

What is in a Label?

I am conscious of the controversy that surrounds the concept of labelling. However, labels can have their place. Labelling can have a role in putting into words the symptoms we experience. In general medicine, patients are easily labelled as having multiple sclerosis, (MS), for example. Similarly, the label of bipolar in psychiatry is no different. Nowadays, the term 'diagnosis' seems a softer and more preferred language for making sense of health abnormalities.

Once diagnosed, I was mindful to not solely focus on being branded. My aim centred on how I was going to manage life with a mental health diagnosis, but still have a meaningful existence. Like a Heinz baked bean tin, many shoppers look beyond the label and choose the shop's own brand, especially these days with the cost-of-living crisis!

Often, the product tastes no different. This philosophy was applied to me. I am no lesser a person just because the word bipolar has been added to 'Anna.'

As you will know by now, I see my diagnosis as my shadow. It can go from the jet-black end of a paint colour chart, passing through the grey samples, to the brightest of whites. As you read on, you will see the explicit characteristics of what equates to the varying shades of my shadow.

Like that baked bean tin, bipolar delivers precisely what it says on the tin! It comes under the mood disorder umbrella. I've often needed an umbrella to shade and shelter me from the blinding white manias and the downpours of black depression.

Both mood episodes are poles apart. At one end of the pole is the mood of mania, and at the other, depression. The term bipolar articulates these extreme disruptions to mood, behaviour and thoughts. In the early days of my diagnosis, I would often be told by friends: "Highs and lows in mood are just a natural feature in anyone's life." They soon realised that my highs and lows were somewhat different. The extremes get in the way of relationships, work, and basic daily living, causing disruption. Magnification, is the best word that describes my then uncontrolled mood pattern.

Black and white are the two colours that resemble the clear-cut moods of my bipolar experience. I lacked a dimmer switch for quite some time, but I promise by the end of this book, I did find an 'electrician.' While waiting for this 'electrician', I lived my late teenage years through to my late twenties, not knowing if the days, weeks or months ahead were going to be lived in the world of 'Tigger' or 'Eeyore.' Without that 'electrician', I never established that middle ground of grey, which is where the character of 'Piglet' best fits. Going back to my driving analogy, my headlights would either be on full beam, or turned off entirely.

'Tigger' times

In my 'Tigger' days, I have often been likened to an excitable hyperactive Duracell bunny, bouncing around at high speed with an outpouring of limitless energy. During these times, I have felt elated, feeling like I could fly higher than the Empire State Building, with invincibility shining through. When 'Tigger', sleep is not a necessity.

Life and soul of a gathering is another phrase used to describe my character. Friends and colleagues have also often been baffled at how I managed to fit everything in. Speaking fast is another trait my loved ones think of when describing historic manic episodes. On recollection, I have had so much zest for life, committing to all opportunities. I would often have a flurry of ideas, being naive to life's limitations. When at my most manic, grandiosity has featured. For 'Tigger', money also has been known to grow on trees, and outlandish spending has boosted the retail economy. This is an invisible illness, but I have many possessions that are physical reminders of my manic spending moments. Not to mention the six suitcases and cordless hoovers purchased when on a spree!

Being in the company of 'Tigger' one minute, and then learning of 'Eeyore's' intensive care admissions has been hard for family and friends to process. The drastic shifts in mood have been extraordinary. What goes up, must inevitably come down. I have often looked at paragliders and seen for myself that they cannot stay up forever. Coming down with such a bump can inflict grief, yearning for the loss of not sustaining that high. Before stopping medication or making any attempt to get high again, I must remember that my highs are so short-lived.[6] It is worth noting, that I have never experienced a high without a substantial crash thereafter. As the years went on, I tended to present more on

---

[6] When I talk about 'highs', this is by no means linked to illegal drug use. It is associated with bipolar, commenting on the elevation of mood experienced.

the lower side, and my diagnosis moved more towards bipolar type II. The two types differ. With type II, people are more likely to experience less severe manias, with the highs being classed in the bracket of hypomania. The depressive episodes are often more frequent and severe.

'Eeyore' episodes

When living at the other end of the spectrum as 'Eeyore', I could be mistaken for Victor Meldrew, allowing no room for optimism! When like this, it can be gruelling to get through each hour of the day. I remember feeling retired from life, running on empty. When in such episodes, my existence has been questioned. At times, I have quite frightfully been absorbed by tormenting suicidal thoughts. Feeling like I had no future or purpose helped fuel my feelings of hopelessness and self-worthlessness.

When at my lowest, a brain fog would cloud and engulf my thought processes and judgment. The darkest cloud, nimbostratus, would cover my sky, thick enough to prevent any sunlight from peering in. I often felt the colour had gone out of my life, leaving me to exist in a dark pit. Even breathing seemed like an enormous effort. I felt unplugged. That 'electrician' has been in high demand. My eyes have given a lot away, being expressionless. When 'Eeyore', they have a transparency that makes them look sluggish and lifeless. Agitation, consistent negativity, along with failing to get any pleasure from an activity, are all warning signs of me entering an 'Eeyore' phase. My bedhead curly hair and dot-to-dot spotty skin have also been indicators of me being in a low episode.

Along similar lines to the paraglider metaphor, what goes down, must come up. Miners cannot stay down the coal mine forever. Therefore, one can conclude that neither state is sustainable, but both can be so destructive to the everyday functioning of life.

My cognitive analytical therapist, (CAT), focused on taming the highs and mellowing the lows. My recovery journey's focal point has been to strive to exist in the grey, softening the colours of the brightest of whites and darkest of blacks on that gradient colour chart.

The 'Tigger' and 'Eeyore' symptoms noted, are relevant to me. Every bipolar patient is unique, we all present differently. Once you have seen one bipolar patient, you have seen one bipolar patient. This is not too dissimilar with any other health condition, but there is always some common ground.

Other bipolar sufferers may agree with me that when in an episode, we feel like strangers in our own bodies. Now balanced, I find it difficult to comprehend the person that I talk about in this book as myself. Episodes have lasted from a couple of weeks to months. My local psychiatric team never saw me in full-swing mania. Those days preceded my first dealings with the service.

Labels can be helpful, but they can also be confusing and damaging. They can feel like they define you. Mental health diagnoses are never clear-cut, and often psychiatrists have differing opinions. Psychiatrists only see you for a limited time. Over the years, I found it hard to articulate myself in a pressurised review setting. Therefore, often their assessments haven't been based on a true reflection and representation of how I was at the time. When stabilisation was difficult to establish, it was natural for healthcare professionals to blur the lines and hand out incorrect diagnoses, causing an uneasy and distressing time.

Before I was discharged from the service in July 2022,

my psychiatrist thankfully persuaded me to have a course of psychotherapy. The neurodevelopmental disability, autism spectrum disorder, (ASD), is a label that was interestingly loosely assigned to me at the late age of thirty-three, when engaging in this psychotherapy. It has since been agreed with my psychiatrist that I fall into the bipolar bracket, with additional high-functioning autistic traits.

The autistic spectrum is broad and traits can easily be mistaken for other mental health conditions. Having psychotherapy, helped my team to explain my presentation during my many hospitalisations, as opposed to the other labels that had been added into the mix. This additional diagnosis has helped me, my family and my psychiatric team understand 'me' a lot more. It was no surprise to Mum.

Girls are commonly known to be diagnosed with it late in life, being able to disguise it more easily. I wouldn't say my signs and symptoms are typical of those that you instantly associate with autism. Mine are more related to delayed cognitive and learning skills, difficulty with sleeping, adapting to change and organisational processing.

I have chosen not to go down a lengthy formal assessment of this, my journey has been long enough.

Having this awareness, has however, given me food for thought and something to work with.

This unmistakably goes hand in hand with my documented mental health struggles and bipolar diagnosis, as the two intertwine and merge. The management of my autistic traits has naturally become easier to control and challenge, as my general mental wellbeing has been mastered.

"Success is the ability to go from one failure to another with no loss of enthusiasm."

-Winston Churchill.[7]

---

[7] Quotation by the late bipolar sufferer, Winston Churchill. Taken from Bertolucci, D. (2012) *'Love Your Life'* London: Hardie Grant Books, pp.192. Retrieved September 8, 2019.

Surviving the Setbacks

This chapter comes with an alert, being the most turbulent part of my story.

As we were warned, there have been many highs and lows since leaving the secure unit. Family, friends and some healthcare professionals have likened me to 'a cat with nine lives.' Unfortunately, while healthcare professionals and I were desperately trying to get a grip on my bipolar, some lives were inevitably lost from my 'cat bank.'

It is important to remember that relapse is a key part of recovery. Even though my journey has been somewhat long and relentless, it has been extremely repetitive. In this chapter, I am therefore not going to talk about each crisis I have endured. The most poignant moments of my uphill journey will be exposed. Intentionally, I have spared the intricate detail of each documented setback, allowing some personal privacy.

After being flown back from the secure unit, I was directly transferred to our local psychiatric ward. Over three years, (from 2013), I had four major crises and felt destroyed by mental illness. The skill of kangarooing was adopted.

Every time I seemed to be recovering, I tended to push over into an episode of hypomania, then soon crashed back down, causing irrational thoughts and behaviour. Throughout this period, we were struggling to find a treatment plan that suited me.

Taking one day at a time was an impossible task. What was I supposed to do with that one day? A whole day would fill me with dread. I was unable to be comfortable in my skin and company, finding the prospect of an empty day daunting. When at my worst, my psychiatric care team would check in with me hourly, suggesting things for me to do to keep myself safe by signposting.

Time seemed to stand still when I was hospitalised. Hours, days, nights and weekends merged. I seemed governed by medication and ward rounds, welcomed visitations, trials off the ward and what was for dinner! This dull way of living was difficult to accept, when I knew everybody's lives were continuing outside of the four walls of my hospital room. As I experienced, you don't have to physically be behind bars to feel imprisoned. I just struggled to break free from this rut, as I sadly wasn't reaching a position where I could even begin to try and recover, hence all the setbacks. I was desperate to allow the light to come in and for me to get better, but didn't feel I had the means.

(Setback one was how my story started; events leading to my transfer to the secure unit, explained in chapter one and two)

Setback two, at the end of May 2013

During a phased discharge from our local psychiatric ward, I faced setback number two. I struggled with this as I had lived such a manic life for so long pre-diagnosis. When leaving the ward structure, I kept crashing. Although I may have been physically free, I still felt mentally trapped in my very own prison.

Desperately trying to chase that high, I often forgot about the enormity of recurring manias. On reflection, I was only on an extremely high dose of antipsychotic medication. This alone didn't seem to hold me. My mood reflected a camel's hump, causing me to revert to my 'Tigger' characteristics. 'Tigger' finally lost its bounce and in walked 'Eeyore', causing a suicide attempt. An ICU admission was the consequence.

Setback three, in November 2014

Managing to nurse through a phased return on a medical rehabilitation ward, I was back in my nursing blues. While nursing in this area, I was headhunted to transfer to the nurse specialism of oncology. This was the perfect area of nursing for me, I was excelling. Daily, I continued to battle with the debilitating drowsiness of Quetiapine.

Although my medication was often referred to as my life support machine, unfortunately, the side effects outweighed the benefits. With daily life and work becoming impossible to get through, I saw no option but to take myself off this medication to function. Over time, 'Tigger' made another appearance, and then 'Eeyore' was not far behind. Setback three was experienced, resulting in a further ICU admission.

Sadly, I had been verbalising my medication struggles, but sometimes patient experiences aren't always understood. The grieving process showed its face again. I knew what lay ahead, another lengthy psychiatric admission.

Setback four, at the end of September 2015

Ten months on, with no periods of absence, I got promoted to a band six senior nurse in oncology. During this time, some marvellous family friends orchestrated a second opinion in the UK, Harley Street. This was backed by my incredible local family GP, who has been a pillar of support throughout my entire journey and continues to be.

My family and I were exhausted from the relentless relapse cycle that had gone before. The professor I saw, who specialised in bipolar, believed I had textbook bipolar. He put me on the gold standard treatment. Unfortunately, I also remained on such high doses of Quetiapine. Induced drowsiness continued to be an ongoing battle.

Once again, I stopped all medication, as I was struggling to function. The usual characteristics were displayed, 'Tigger' was in fine form. This, like any other manic episode, could not be sustained and the wall came tumbling down. There was a further suicidal setback.

The creation of an emergency action plan was essential, I was like a revolving door. In times of crisis, I was often helpless. Having a crisis care plan as a point of reference, allowed me to maintain a degree of responsibility and control for my treatment. It would normally be visual, in the form of a flow chart. It consisted of a list of emergency contacts, medications, signs and symptoms that indicate that others may need to take charge and treatment preferences.

When I went through all the documented setbacks that are in this chapter, this emergency action plan was worn out with usage. I am happy to say it has now safely been filed away for many years.

Lightening of that jet-black shadow was about to happen. Due to my needs, I was transferred to a more intensive community mental health team. I was saved from facing setback five.

In the spring of 2017, I was admitted to hospital as a result of having to come off Lithium due to kidney function. I became very unwell due to this, causing me to enter a severe depressive episode as a consequence. It was this admission that encouraged me to take stock of things. Resigning from nursing and moving back home post-discharge, were the main adjustments. 2017 was a very tough year for me, but later proved beneficial and productive for my recovery.

Me and My Shadow

When hospitalised, I felt like I was on show. I remember getting distressed at the constant analysis. The below scrutiny was gruelling to get through. Although, I was very much aware that this was part and parcel of being under the care of healthcare professionals.

- "Is she high?"
- "Is she low?"
- "How is her personality affected?"
- "Does she accept things?"
- "Is she sleeping?"
- "What medication should we change?"

It is so refreshing to now be naturally living with little assessment and judgment, or only when necessary.

Throughout my journey, I have been under numerous community psychiatric nurses (CPNs) and psychiatrists, this has caused disruption. A high turnover of staff in healthcare is inevitable, but it can feel like an upheaval, having to get used to a different care team over and over again. It takes time to build up trust, get to know your team, go over common ground and continuously relive mental health history. I was fortunate to be under one remarkable nurse, who won nurse of the year locally. I was proud to have nominated her. As I started to become more balanced, sounding less like a broken record, therapeutic relationships were a lot easier to establish and engage in.

My cyclic whirlwind of the past few years could be likened to the development of a baby. Over the years of trying to reach a balanced and well Anna, I managed to: roll myself over, conquer the art of sitting up unaided, upgrade to crawling, attempt to stand and furniture walk. Then, the minute I let go, I hit the carpet with a crash.

This cyclic pattern became consuming and exhausting. Another way of looking at it is like being on a treadmill. Here I would be pounding away, not being able to keep the pace up. When I got back on at a slower pace, I would soon go full steam ahead, starting the chaotic approach to recovery again. Part of my problem was my desperation to run away and shut the door on bipolar. Rushing to get out of each relapse wasn't helpful. It has been so hard to be a patient patient!

Lack of acceptance and holding much anger for the diagnosis, held my successful recovery back. When in mania, I have been told I was dismissive of anyone referring to my mental health. I believed I was on top of the world and just wanted to get on with my life without constant reference to it. When like this, I didn't think there was anything wrong with me and felt people were just stopping me from being happy. It has been confusing to differentiate between the meanings of happy and high.

Having spoken with healthcare professionals, meeting other sufferers and reading some articles, it is a well-known fact that reaching a prolonged course of stability can take years. I am no different. Finding the right medication, gaining the correct level of insight and accepting the mental health card dealt, has taken years to achieve.

Sadly, however, I believe that I wouldn't have had suicide attempts two, three and four, if these three components had fallen into place in a timelier manner. Maturing into the illness is what I have most certainly done, just like a good wine or cheese!

Prevention is important with early intervention being key. This rings true with a lot of illnesses. In the earlier days, the care I received was not always the most efficient or effective, with intervention happening more after a crisis rather than before. This is not a blaming session at the care system. Mental health is tricky to control but thankfully, the team I was later under adopted a different and more proactive approach.

Albeit late, once autistic traits were identified, my psychiatrist understood me a lot better. We both now fully grasp how I function, which is the vital ingredient for a successful therapeutic relationship. I am proud to state that I have never lost more 'cat lives' and I never intend to. I am still 'meowing and purring' through life! I am appreciative to be a survivor of suicide.

Kissing a Few Frogs

Like boyfriends, you have to kiss a few frogs to find 'Mr Right' in terms of finding the most suitable treatment. I had to use a trial-and-error approach with medication to find out what worked best for me. Exploring different treatment regimes is a long-haul process. It has taken seven years to find a clean combination of psychotropics and mood stabilisers.

Relapses are part and parcel of the illness. I have had to accept that the odd admission is part of one's life. Transferring to the new community mental health team caused much apprehension. I was tentative to handle yet more change. Continuous tweaking, crisis intervention and close monitoring from this intensive outreach team contributed to the eventual successful management of my bipolar symptoms.

They have worked closely with me, increasing or decreasing contact as per my requirements. I have been hospitalised many times under this team, some for long periods. These admissions proved productive as they avoided further crises. This intensive community care was provided predominantly during my break from nursing in 2017.

There is so much more to mental health recovery than just chemicals and popping pills. Nonetheless, medication does have its place. The professor of bipolar, whom I was fortunate to see on Harley Street, once told me: "You can't treat bipolar with just willpower alone Anna." He was a strong believer that medication is the scaffolding, with everything else being built on thereafter.

My brain required to be chemically balanced before other holistic therapies were entertained. I was not to beat myself up for the attempts made on my life. He fully understood why these had happened, considering how long it took for me to find a compatible treatment regime.

On my mental health drive, I have occasionally taken a wrong turn when making decisions to stop and start medication. This felt like the last resort, which is known to be bipolar's big cardinal sin. I can assure you I am not alone in doing this. For me, this has largely been down to four key reasons:

1) When I have previously felt better, I often decided that I didn't need medication.

2) When I have felt overmedicated.
3) To chase that high.
4) Due to ghastly side effects.

Psychiatric medication comes with some horrid side effects. I have specifically endured: oversedation, increasing appetite, significant weight gain, restless legs, tremors, consistent thirst and a metal taste to name but a few. At one period, I was taking fifteen tablets nightly, this was hard going.

Finally, in my twenty-ninth year, I was in luck, and I am now on what I call a clean regime. Sodium Valproate, which is a mood stabiliser and Quetiapine, an antipsychotic, equates for the right cocktail mix for me. When clinically required, I also have periodic use of a specific antidepressant, Mirtazapine, and night sedation.

The transforming decision to have my antipsychotic administered at regular time intervals throughout the day has been effective. This has avoided the debilitating sedative effects and the peaks and troughs in mood. I now use my insight to my advantage. If I recognise a warning sign, I request an as-required prescription and self-medicate appropriately, along with attempting to change a lifestyle behaviour.

For over five years, I have been fortunate to have sustained a long period of wellness, remaining on the same treatment with no chopping and changing.

Yes, I accept that my weight is not where I would like it to be, but no hospitalisations have been required during this time. Therefore, my weight is a small price to pay for stability, prompting me to take the rough with the smooth. Perseverance with diet and exercise has contributed to me deflating somewhat from my secure unit days!

Diabetics need insulin or tablets to maintain their blood sugars. In parallel, I need mood stabilisers and other psychiatric medication to keep me on the right track. There is no difference. Medication is like a pair of glasses. Bipolar distorted my vision of life. Like spectacles, medication allows me to see more clearly. Medication can also be likened to running shoes. To run a marathon, an athlete requires a decent pair of trainers to provide cushioning to soften the impact.

By taking the clean medication regime that we eventually found, I think and act more slowly, ride a smoother journey and cope with whatever life throws at me, weathering inevitable storms.

When working through my diagnosis as I drove along that mental health road, I was fortunate enough to build on top of medication and undergo intensive CAT therapy. No, I wasn't placed in a room stroking cats! It was time-limited therapy that provided me with a platform to look at the way I think, feel and behave. It complemented the already established cognitive behavioural therapy, (CBT), skills and family therapy sessions I had acquired and attended.

My therapist and I sketched mind maps and traced traits of my illness right back to childhood and life experiences. The grief and trauma I experienced as a child was a big avenue we explored and worked through. Also knowing that my late Dad suffered from manic depression was fascinating to note and discuss.

There are many days when I would have appreciated the chance to sit down with him and compare our Bowditch bipolar brains! I have also been able to heal from traumatic memories that my mental health ordeal has caused, by completing a course of eye movement desensitization and reprocessing therapy (EMDR).

Recognising the busyness of my childhood has helped me to see where the constant striving, thriving and importance of achieving goals came from. The writing was on the wall. This is one of my driving reasons for writing this book. Life isn't all about achievements and trying to rise to social pressures. Doing what you can, and being good enough is paramount. Mum never pushed me. As I was a slow developer, I pushed myself to have such a strong work ethic. I then did every extra-curricular school activity available. This was because I had the opportunity, and most importantly, I got so much enjoyment out of it all.

Our childhood was full, largely to compensate for the loss of my dear Dad. Being still was a rarity, with me displaying manic traits as I approached early adulthood.

Striving to achieve the greys on my colour chart and operate the dimmer switch that my 'electrician' fitted has allowed me to tread down a different path. My CAT therapist also helped me walk through the untrodden grass to mark new territory, finding routes that are not heavily stricken by the unhealthy shades of my shadow.

In relinquishing the old me, I have explored new avenues to develop the new me. Family and friends will be aware that I have no sense of direction, believing everywhere I face is North! CAT therapy, however, has helped me to get a grip on the compass and navigate the route to my recovery.

Finding balance will be a lifelong endeavour. There is a fine line between not feeling too flattened but at the same time, achieving a life that has a level of acceptable excitement. I am striving to be that 'spirit level' with the bubble in the middle.

Most people as they mature want to avoid the colour grey, especially when it comes down to hair colour! Grey is what I will always be striving for in life. I envisage it as the mutual colour that sits away from the jet black of depression and the brightest of whites that is mania. The colour grey is therefore the bubble in my 'spirit level.' This journey has redefined me and persuaded me to be content with the grey and consequently well 'Anna', who sits quite nicely in the middle.

Being 'Grey'

What constitutes a grey Anna?

When grey, my eyes are alive.

When grey, my skin is flawless. It no longer screams out for someone to join the dots of spots.

When grey, my often commented-upon smile radiates through.

When grey, I function, full stop.

When grey, I am in control of everyday things.

When grey, I no longer overspend.

When grey, I have been described as having a calm aura around me.

When grey, I am more productive in life.

Me and My Shadow

When grey, I gain genuine enjoyment from doing things.

When grey, I get and feel tired with my sleep hygiene existing.

When grey, my fitness improves, being able to stick at things, but not overdoing it.

When grey, I can be still, not feeling the need to plan for the next adventure. I am content and satisfied in my own skin.

When grey, I comprehend that Rome wasn't built in a day, not feeling the need to conquer everything right at that moment.

When grey, my black and white thinking is no more, therefore my thoughts and plans are no longer extreme.

When grey, overthinking and catastrophising are toxic

thought behaviours of the past.

When grey, I cope with life's natural highs and lows like anyone else.

When grey, I am happy to take responsibility for myself and my mental health.

When grey, I can be told and take on board advice from healthcare professionals, family and friends.

When grey, I am satisfied with being good enough. I accept the compromises that my diagnosis has encouraged me to make.

When grey, I manage to hold down my nursing role, continuing to deliver high standards of care and am my old reliable self.

When grey, in social situations, the euphoria of the event doesn't carry me into a hypomanic state. The good time stops accordingly.

Me and My Shadow

When grey, I am consistently balanced, making 'Tigger' and 'Eeyore' redundant.

When grey, I'm a joy to live with according to Mum. Disagreements are few and far between.

When grey, irritability is not present.

The most liberating three greys of all are:
1) When grey, the difference is, that if and when I feel myself going high or low, I stop and communicate.
2) When grey, I am balanced enough to swallow the shame I have experienced over the years, feeling empowered to speak openly about my mental health.
3) When grey, I tentatively live, avoiding being complacent in my daily living. I am mindful of making a mistake and pushing over into a manic or depressive state. Managing my bipolar has taken so long to establish, therefore, I am naturally nervous to undo all my hard work. Having a

constant awareness of my bipolar shadow, which I liken to a parrot on my shoulder, prevents me from off-roading.

Finding and walking this grey path towards recovery, taught me to think carefully about the 'Anna' that was worth returning to. I was conscious that I had been so used to living in an unwell state for so long, that I may have confused illness with normality. I was keen to learn from what I have been through, avoiding automatically going back to old ways.

"Life doesn't come with a manual; it comes with a mother."

-Unknown.[8]

---

[8] Quotation by an Anonymous Author. Found from a general Google internet search on the importance of mothers, displayed on multiple pages. Original source not known. Retrieved October 18, 2020.

Anna Bowditch

Everybody Needs a 'Sidecar'

No mother or parent for that matter, would want to see their child go through the mental health turmoil that became my twenties. Mum's life had to be put on hold to ensure that mine could continue. Mum can have me to thank for being the root cause of her fifty shades of grey hair and increased wrinkles! It hasn't just been my turmoil to endure. Mum has been driving alongside me in her 'sidecar', being my rock, picking up the pieces. We have suffered both individually and together. We've seen this journey through, drawing strength from one another.

It was Mum who:

- Featured heavily in my psychosis, along with close family.
- Had to watch her daughter become unrecognisable during my psychotic period.
- Retrieved a suicide note from under her pillow, with a police officer by her side.
- Watched from the hard shoulder as I was flown off to the UK and sectioned.

- Listened to the label being assigned to me during our first ward round.
- Commuted daily across London to visit me.
- Has always been in ICU by my bedside following a crisis.
- Had to accept that hospital admissions became part and parcel of both our lives.
- When in hospital locally, visited me more than once a day. She repeatedly accepted that there was no improvement from one day to the next. Her car knew its way to our local mental health facility.
- Rightfully shed many tears when visiting time ended and came home to an empty house, missing my Dad's presence to talk things through.
- After the initial commencement of psychiatric medication, saw me balloon in weight, like an inflatable mattress.
- Saw me presenting as unwell, always getting the same answer back: "I am fine!"
- Has supported me to achieve all that I have pre-, during and post-diagnosis.
- Has never given up hope for my recovery even

though her petrol tank of hope was very nearly empty. Any hope I had held had dissipated long ago.

The list could easily be more comprehensive, but I just wanted to create a picture of the stupendous woman she is. There is much guilt I carry when considering Mum had a hard enough job raising three children single-handedly as a result of becoming a young widow.

Just when she thought she was over the worst and had got all of us to adulthood, my mental health journey was added to her load.

When I was recovering, Mum took on the role of a mirror. She was trying to reflect back to me what was being portrayed to her. Sometimes, she would see chaotic behaviour, fast speech, agitation, and insomnia; 'Tigger.' At other times, sloth-like behaviour, duvet days and lifeless eyes would be noticed; 'Eeyore.' The onus was on her to try and be the goalie and catch the warning signs.

I have spoken about how lonely this journey has been for me, but the loneliness Mum must have felt is incomprehensible. There was no manual providing guidance.

The daughter she once had an unbreakable bond with became unidentifiable. During what was a very long storm, she was the umbrella sheltering me in every downpour. This has since allowed us to experience, soak up, be grateful for and mindful of the rainbows that randomly now appear.

Time is the currency best spent. This was said by a family friend when delivering a eulogy at a funeral. Going through what Mum and I have endured together, has encouraged me to not take our special relationship for granted.

We are very much into our experiences now, investing in valuable time together. Thankfully, our bond is stronger than ever as a consequence of the storms that we have weathered. I now endeavour to make a good ending despite a dodgy middle.

During periods of wellness, I have realised how blessed I have been to have a 'sidecar.' Not everybody is fortunate to have one. Mum has been my advocate, giving me the strength to drive out of the dark tunnel into the light. I believe she got her resilience and strength to cope with my diagnosis from being a young widow. Our relationship naturally suffered when I struggled to get to grips with managing my bipolar. Mum felt like she had lost her daughter.

Being told by her on my thirtieth birthday that she had finally got her daughter back, was the best birthday present I could have wished for. It was a jewel-like moment that I will treasure. Genuinely, I wouldn't have been able to get my shadow into that subtle shade of grey without her. I blend beautifully into her tasteful Guernsey cottage, where the colour scheme is; grey!

We must remember that mental ill health doesn't just affect the person who is diagnosed with the condition. Significant others are impacted too. Although I was very much on my own journey, it was Mum and my immediate family who were my main spectators watching from the autocross race barriers.

The other valuable members of my trackside support team consisted of my two brothers and auntie: Tim, Matt and my Auntie Joan. They were my bolsters, ensuring a more comfortable ride was experienced. They witnessed my turbulent journey from the sidelines. Having no expertise in car mechanics, they felt as helpless as Mum. They visited me in hospital, as and when they could. They later told me they were often filled with dread every time the phone rang, being fearful of what crisis had materialised.

Watching me not get better was the hardest thing. By providing secondary support to Mum, they cushioned the impact that my illness was directly having on her. I am eternally grateful for this. My sibling and immediate family relationships naturally suffered. It has been a relief for such relationships to begin to mend, now wellness has been reached and sustained.

I now hand the microphone over to Mum, my 'sidecar.'

Anna Bowditch

Mum's the Word

Anna has invited me to contribute to her story. I will share my parent's perspective of what it has been like to be Anna's 'sidecar', supporting her as she navigated her journey. In the words of Audrey Hepburn: "The best thing to hold onto in life is each other." [9] That is exactly what Anna and I did throughout her turbulent twenties.

I have witnessed the obstacles that have got in her way, paused at some zebra crossings and faced some road closures with her. What we both hold onto is that we never hit a dead end, even if it felt like it.

I believe the traditional wedding vow, 'in sickness and in health', should automatically apply when you become a parent too. Anna's family and friends were as shocked as I was to learn of her unfortunate diagnosis. I had no hesitation in driving alongside her on what was a ten-year expedition. I still loved her even though she wasn't so loveable, matching a quote I saw from the Dalai Lama which was on a piece of

---

[9] Quotation by Audrey Hepburn. Taken from Bertolucci, D. (2012) *'Love Your Life'* London: Hardie Grant Books, pp. 72. Retrieved November 15, 2020.

wood nailed to a tree on a beach in Tulum: "Love is the absence of judgement." Unconditional love bound us together. My desperation drove me to get my daughter back. Anna had been lost for some time, and so had our wonderful relationship.

I will be going over some ground already covered by Anna, as there is a natural crossover.

Childhood

Anna's formative years will be discussed, to create a picture of her pre-diagnosis. Anna was one of triplets, being the youngest by one minute. She was born into a family with an older brother of three years. We were a tight-knit family. She also has three half-siblings. Anna's bereavement began at a young age, which she notes in chapter three. Experiencing all these losses by the age of fifteen had more of a significant impact than we first realised.

Despite the sadness in Anna's early years, she squeezed everything out of life. Learning and gaining grade eight flute, dancing in all genres that the dancing school had to offer and performing in musicals and pantomimes, were just some of the activities Anna participated in up to age eighteen.

Being a single parent to three young children was not an easy ride. I did my best to ensure that their childhood was never compromised.

Anna was a late developer academically, but was conscientious. There was a time when transferring Anna to a special needs school was a possibility during her primary to secondary school transitionary years. She worked tirelessly to stop this transfer from coming to fruition. Mastering things did not come naturally to her. She therefore went above and beyond what was asked of her.

Her exceptional results reflected how hard I watched her work as a parent. My concern has been that perhaps all this hard work contributed to a form of burnout.

Our home was a happy one, with her Dad's sense of humour being kept alive. Anna's beaming smile and radiant personality were often commented upon. From a very young age, Anna only had one career focus, nursing. She had expressed that, due to her experience of loss, she wanted to care for people and contribute to their health journeys. It echoes her empathetic and compassionate nature.

The holidays I was able to take the family on as a

single parent influenced her desire to see the world. I am very proud of the outreach work Anna has participated in over the years in less developed countries. Our relationship was admired by all who knew us. Anna never went through the teenage grump and grunt period. I couldn't have asked for a better daughter.

Looking back, perhaps the difficulty we had with Anna's sleep as a child could explain her fast and active brain. We had to rock her over the room join in her buggy to get her to sleep. She later took up head banging from toddler age to early teenage years to tire herself out.

Anna first showed signs of mood disturbances at age seventeen. Things escalated gradually from then on. Anna and our family were embarking on what would be a significant mental health journey.

Living with Anna pre-diagnosis

Manic and chaotic living crept in. 'Tigger' had entered our household. As manic living became her norm, living with Anna proved as challenging as when I became a widow. Our relationship had disintegrated. She was erratic in everything she engaged with, becoming unrecognisable. I had to learn to love a stranger.

It was seven years from when the first signs presented to her being given a diagnosis. If I'd known then what I know now, red flags would have been raised much sooner. I want this chapter to reach out to parents who are going through similar experiences. Mania left undiagnosed, and therefore untreated, can sometimes push someone into a psychotic state, which unfortunately happened to Anna.

Unbeknown to me, Anna periodically lost contact with reality. She had difficulty recognising what was real and what was not. She had become delusional, paranoid and falsely believed that her bank accounts had been hacked by myself and some of the family. I had become her enemy and the beast of her psychosis.

At the time, I did not know this presentation meant Anna was psychotic, having never heard of the term before. Things had significantly changed. Arguments became a common feature. This was out of character. I just put this down to delayed puberty.

It was heartrending to learn later that I was at the core of my daughter's psychosis. Even though there was no truth in it, I naturally worried about what people who learnt of Anna's psychosis must have thought of me.

Supporting my late husband, Peter, through his manic depressive episodes, should have stood me in good stead for Anna's later presentation. However, Peter differed from Anna, his hypomanic states were never as heightened. He thankfully never became psychotic and ran more on the depressive side. It is all about early intervention, but you need the knowledge to raise the alarm.

With hindsight, I would have pulled 'Anna and Annie' off the 'dual carriageway', moving them both over to the hard shoulder much sooner. I just wasn't aware it was a 'dual carriageway' that Anna was driving on.

Thursday 25th April 2013, D-Day

Anna made a serious attempt on her life on this day, but it was vital for this to have come to a head. The mental health service needed to become the driver of 'Anna' urgently. She had struggled for too long on her own. Opening the door to a police officer that day was unexpected.

Retrieving a suicide note from under my pillow left me numb, speechless and devastated. Anna had been detained and was being transferred to our local psychiatric ward. This was to provide a place of safety. Later learning that Anna was to be flown to a psychiatric secure unit in London, was very traumatic.

Having had time to assess Anna, her psychiatrist in the UK made contact with me. She shared her clinical opinion, explaining that she believed Anna was psychotic and discussed the diagnosis of bipolar. The pieces of the jigsaw were beginning to fit.

This diagnosis permitted me to feel relieved, allowing us as a family to come together and embrace what was to come. It was going to be a new beginning for Anna, rather than the ending that she had planned for that day. The transfer had a profound effect on Anna and those close to her.

I very nearly lost my daughter to suicide. She had reached a crisis point before there was any engagement with the mental health service. If Anna had taken her life on this day, she would not be here now, contributing to that much-needed mental health conversation. The reality is, she would have left us, without us knowing that she would have had a treatable and manageable mental health illness.

Even though she made further attempts on her life, thankfully, she is now well and has accomplished and continues to accomplish so much. The further attempts can largely be put down to the length of time it took to find the correct medication regime, insufficient care at times and Anna not accepting the condition. Anna has overcome mental illness and the unfortunate stigma that has come with it. I am bursting with pride and am grateful to be asked to contribute to her memoir.

It is a given that a book of this kind would have helped us all as a family immensely.

We attend presentations together to continue Anna's recovery and enrich our mental health awareness. At a suicide prevention presentation, it was comforting to sit shoulder-to-shoulder next to my daughter, a survivor of suicide. Some people in the room weren't as lucky. Imagining my life without Anna was and is unthinkable.

The journey

Anna's relentless journey has been exhausting, draining and heartbreaking. Visiting Anna daily in hospital, both in the UK and in Guernsey, became my life. There was a prolonged time when I never saw an improvement, but for Anna, I had to visibly show hope for her recovery. Seeing the side effects that the varying treatments inflicted on her was difficult to observe. The psychiatric care team were not always seeing my daughter for who she was.

When unwell, she was so misunderstood. It was illness causing her to present how she was. This was upsetting, as I knew Anna's nature differed greatly when she wasn't under the spell of mental illness.

Over the years, I took Anna off the ward for short periods as her leave allowed and assisted her with trialling overnight homestays. More importantly, I regularly attended ward rounds, family therapy sessions, mindfulness and a carer's course to facilitate Anna's holistic recovery. Patience was the biggest virtue that we both had to acquire to invest in her sustained positive mental health outcome.

During the crux of Anna's journey, there was never a time when I stopped worrying about her wellbeing. A particular example of this was in 2016, when we just happened to be travelling around Asia on separate tours.

Anna was travelling with an organised group of fellow single travellers; I was travelling with friends. Ironically, our itineraries meant we were in the same location, Luang Prabang in Laos, for one day. We managed to meet up for a meal together. Anna was the most manic I had seen her. She has got a disturbing photo of her out in Laos as a stark reminder. She decided to keep this photo as a motivational attempt for her to never return to a manic state again.

It transpired that the mania was later put down to: a combination of time differences, a demanding travel itinerary, three weeks of minimal sleep and a disturbed medication routine.

Seeing Anna presenting this way left me heartbroken. Anna insisted that I resume with my separate travel trip, this being a clear example of her poor insight. I was mindful of what I was going to be coming back to on my return. Knowing that she was that unwell, in a country and culture that was unknown to her, caused much angst and worry.

What could I do?

A local lengthy hospitalisation was the outcome on Anna's return. Although this was a scary time for Anna, she often talks about how much this has taught her. It did bring an element of the shock factor. There was a realisation that a psychiatric hospital admission could have materialised out there, which doesn't bear thinking about.

Suicide is often seen as an act of weakness and a choice. I think otherwise. When conversing with Anna, she has always said that she never wanted to end her life but felt it was the only way to end the turmoil. I cannot begin to imagine the pain she endured to make such attempts on her life. To have watched her overcome all this is remarkable.

Rainbows became our mother-and-daughter thing. When Anna was on timed leave, a rainbow would often appear, signifying better things to come. Rainbows are the after-effect of the dark clouds and downpours that were her past.

What recovery looks like from my perspective

A balanced Anna looks grey to me, blending perfectly into my Guernsey cottage. I am always learning with Anna, especially when she does hit the occasional bump in the road. Anna never has to get as unwell again. Collectively: Anna, her siblings, myself, friends, work colleagues and her psychiatric team have over the years, gained much insight into her triggers, early warning signs, crisis plans and treatment regime.

This awareness has laid down a solid foundation and secure infrastructure for her. This fills me with confidence that we can keep her on track, and nip things in the bud if she shows signs of moving out of the grey.

The journey her diagnosis sent her on, has put mental health on our whole family's agenda. It has brought us all closer together. We are much more open to talking about how we are feeling. Anna's recovery has not been handed to her on a plate. As a parent, I have sat back and watched her persevere, making and accepting compromises. It is because of Anna's sheer determination that when reaching twenty-nine she broke the cycle, exited the roundabout and finally stopped that door from revolving.

We are delighted that she has finally returned to the Anna we love and know. Watching Anna modelling her nursing blues again was a day to remember. In 2019, she got back to doing her thing, she was done with being the patient!

There are days when I forget Anna has a diagnosis, she manages her life so well now. There are also days when I get reminded of what her mental health ordeal has interfered with and stalled. Although pleased for others, it can be hard for both of us to witness Anna's friends who are further ahead in terms of life situations, concerning children, marriage and housing. I encourage Anna not to make comparisons. The life experiences Anna has gained on her journey towards finding positive mental health, have a much stronger value and weight than bricks and mortar!

Overcoming the adversity that we all thought was insurmountable has enabled Anna to be seen as an inspiration by many. You are who you are and I wouldn't change who Anna is. What I would change, is what she went through. We accept the diagnosis, but elements of the journey were rough.

A message to fellow parents/significant others

1) If you have a concern or an inkling that something is astray about the wellbeing of your child, flag it up with a doctor or reach out to the mental health service promptly.

2) Be that physical and emotional 'sidecar' for your child. The ride may not be easy or smooth. You may need suspension to embrace the turbulence.

3) Never give up hope. Hand on heart, there were times when I did not think we were ever going to get Anna back. With patience and countless chopping and changing of treatment, 'Tigger' and 'Eeyore' left the building. My daughter finally walked back into our lives, where she has stayed.

My thanks

Bipolar and Anna's general mental ill health has stolen chapters from both of our lives. I am relieved to say that as well as Anna's life being back on track, our relationship is robust and stronger than ever. Anna was finally returned to the family.

My two dependable sons, Tim and Matt, although across the miles, have kept my 'wheels turning.' Also, I am eternally grateful to my sister, Joan, who hopped into her very own 'car' during crisis points, becoming my 'sidecar!' Also, I would have been lost without precious neighbours and close friends.

I would also like to say a heartfelt thanks to those who Anna leant upon in her hour of need.

Nurses Get Sick Too

Going from a nurse to a patient felt like a radical role reversal. My abrupt awakening of this role transition happened on that D-Day. Autonomy, knowledge, competence and responsibility are attributes that I believe make up a nursing professional's identity. When I walked through the security-locked doors of the psychiatric ward for the first time, I felt like a meek impaired professional.

A psychiatrist who was caring for me conveyed that he had had to section his colleague on the mainland on one occasion. He happened to be a fellow psychiatrist who was in a manic episode of bipolar. This has resonated with me. Healthcare professionals are not immune or invincible to ill health, we can become sick too. I was reassured that this psychiatrist suffering from bipolar did recover and get his career back on track.

My duty as a nurse is to preserve life. When in crisis, I have done the controversial act of trying to end mine. When like this, I felt a burden to everybody, convinced that other people's lives would be better off without me. When I am well and balanced, I realise that this is not so. Ending my life would have destructively ruined many lives within my family as well as my own.

Interestingly, rates of suicide among people with bipolar are twenty to thirty times higher than those without the condition. Moreover, as many as one in five people with bipolar, largely those untreated, end their lives by suicide.[10] This could have so nearly been me, part of a statistic! This helps to explain my suicidal setbacks.

This role reversal was a U-turn I had not expected to take. Before this, I was destined to nurse not to be nursed. As an inpatient, I have internally been frustrated when seeing nurses writing notes, administering medication and conversing with patients. I have instinctively had a running dialogue with myself: "That was and should still be me!"

Naturally, my self-esteem, self-image, self-worth and purpose have historically been distorted, helping me turn into a powerless professional. There is no obvious way of overcoming the conflict that arises between being a patient and a nurse collectively. During an admission, there was a

---

[10] Accessed healthcentral.com on 08/09/24, *10 Signs of Bipolar Disorder; how to tell if your changes in mood signal a mental health disorder*, written by Therese Borchard, updated 08/08/23.

poignant time when I was mistaken for a nurse by one of my fellow psychiatric patients. This patient was correct in an ironic way, believing that I was a nurse in this instance, causing him to approach me and request a care need.

Observing the care I received through the eyes of a nurse, has heightened my awareness for my future nursing practice. Empathy and insight have been enriched. One main observation that became apparent when hospitalised, is how easy it can be for nurses to nurse on auto-pilot. A care task is learnt and repeated over again, but it is new to each patient.

We as nurses need to remember that we know what we are doing, but patients are naive to the clinical skills we practice. It should be our priority to explain and practice with clarity, as if it is the first time of doing the care task.

Although I trained in the general genre of nursing, I always held an interest in mental health. Fascinatedly, I chose my dissertation topic which covered the mental health domain. I had observed my superiors caring for self-harm patients on an acute medical ward placement. My title was, therefore: *A Literature Review on the Attitudes of General Nurses on Acute Medical Wards Towards Deliberate Self-Harm Patients*. I never thought this would become so close to home. Mental ill health can creep up on anyone.

Being a parrot that has fallen off its perch is an analogy that best describes how I feel towards my nursing career. Since the age of five, I always expressed the desire to be a nurse. Like my school days, I gave my training and nursing years my absolute all, having so much passion for my chosen vocation.

Naturally and unfortunately, I required a significant amount of time off since diagnosis. Consequently, I have had to undergo numerous phased returns into all different domains of nursing, undergoing strict screening from occupational therapy to ensure I was fit for practice. The numerous phased returns caused a considerable amount of change to be embraced. Amazingly, after each relapse, I have managed to get back into that blue uniform.

Not returning to the role I once thrived in reiterated how far I had fallen. Bipolar, sadly sent me off-piste from nursing within the field of oncology. I still hold such an interest and passion for this area. It was the right job at the wrong time.

Being within the top three of my nursing cohort, gaining a first-class honours in nursing and getting promoted to a senior staff nurse at a very young age were all so fulfilling. Photocopying day after day on one of my phased returns caused me to feel like bipolar had completely won. Humiliation was a strong feeling that I experienced. Nursing mentors, colleagues and some patients had verbalised over the years that they were surprised that I hadn't trained to be a doctor, and felt strongly that I would go to the top within the nursing field.

Bipolar has impacted and jeopardised the promising nursing career prospects that I once had ahead of me. I had to swallow the pill of working non-clinically, which for a time had its place. Then, I had to be content with moving from a band six to a five, reducing hours to part-time, and taking a salary reduction. All these steps were positive in simplifying life and relieving pressure, but I was struggling with nursing where I was. Mentally, I still had the bar set at returning to the field of oncology.

Not every manager understands mental health. I comprehend that managers have a priority in ensuring that their department is adequately and safely staffed.

Unfortunately, I was unreliable due to such a destructive diagnosis. Before being diagnosed, I was not a sick note, having no time off. My later significant absences were for good reason and could only be assigned to one thing, mental ill health. Nowadays, there does seem to be more educational support for managers surrounding the management of potential mental health issues that employees may present with.

Many nursing colleagues have and continue to say they feel nursing perhaps contributed to my illness. Nursing was not to blame entirely, but some elements didn't help. Before the diagnosis in 2013, due to ward busyness, staff shortages and my conscientious nature, I worked all hours, skipped many breaks and thrived on the manic pace of the shifts.

I lived to work and got into the habit of working on days off and on annual leave to help out. People-pleasing was what I was best at. Like an elastic band, there is only so much stretch in it, mine snapped. Nursing friends without a mental health diagnosis have verbalised that at times, they find the nursing lifestyle challenging for their wellbeing.

The nature of nursing did not complement my undiagnosed and unknown mental health weakness. I was a product of burnout. The increase in work stress contributed to the psychotic state that I entered before I received any mental health intervention. Similar to an elastic band snapping, my body was like an overloaded cargo ship, which inevitably sank.

I shouldn't feel shame when faced with my nursing colleagues, but I sadly do. Guernsey is Guernsey, so confidentiality is a loose term. I do worry that my mental health history has gone before my professional nursing reputation. This upsets me greatly. My brain has been sick, and nursing colleagues should be the professionals who understand and look beyond the label. In certain areas, this has not always been the case.

I have been mentally unwell; this was not a life choice. Contrary to the above, I do have some wonderful nursing colleagues whom I can call my finest friends. They have looked beyond my mental health past. I also acknowledge how hard it must have been for some of my nursing colleagues and nursing friends who had to care for me, forcing them to see me at my most vulnerable.

As well as life in general, my nursing career took a big diversion and in fact, I felt like I had hit a no-entry sign. Once I resigned in 2017, I needed to answer the big question of whether a nursing career was compatible with bipolar. I have had to take responsibility and rethink my career prospects, making reasonable adjustments, but not seeing them as a failure. A former director of nursing I once nursed under, believed that you can nurse with several mental health conditions if managed, bipolar being one of them. Her faith in me, restored my faith in myself. My resignation period lasted eighteen months.

At the beginning of 2019, I swallowed my pride and referred myself to the award-winning small supported employment team, the Guernsey Employment Trust, (GET).[11] This is an invaluable local charity. Trained personnel ensure individuals with both learning disabilities and mental health conditions remain well in employment. They pull on the reins occasionally. This organisation supported me in identifying and applying for an appropriate first return to nursing post. They have since supported me accordingly.

My only regret is, I wish I had been on board with them sooner. A wellness action plan, (WAP), was devised with my efficient employment support officer, (ESO). This is

---

[11] On 07/06/24, the management of GET and Alex Martinson, my ESO, granted written permission for this charity to be explained.

a constant reminder for both myself and my manager of what is needed for me to stay well at work.

Nursing friends have told me that when I resigned, they didn't believe I would return to nursing in a professional capacity, but I was so determined. Pausing nursing, allowed me to acknowledge that I exist as a person that is separate from nursing. Being a nurse does not define me and is not my total identity, it just makes up part of who I am. I now have a healthier relationship with work. On my return after the career break, I couldn't have been working under a more understanding, supportive and encouraging manager and team for my first non-clinical nursing post. This was within clinical governance.

They saw me for my nursing ability rather than my mental health inability. The fact that I got back to nursing in 2019, even though it initially was not where I wanted to be, did not make me any less of a nurse. Only managing part-time hours spoke volumes. It reflected that I was aware of and accepted my limits, which aided me to continue that ongoing slow and steady tortoise recovery.

The slow progression back into the profession was hard. I was a stone's throw away from the wards but was still so far removed from patients. A carrot daily was dangled in front of my nose, and I was unable to reach it. These are natural feelings. The induced slow pace was part and parcel of a sustained and successful return to the profession. The progressive return to nursing was not punitive. It had both my patients' and my own wellbeing at the forefront.

I am now practising as a part-time outpatient nurse locally within the speciality of ophthalmology, being patient-facing. The hours are conducive to my sustained wellness. Over five years, I have had no periods of absence as a result of mental health.

There is some irony in working within the field of ophthalmology when you consider the journey I have been on. When learning to accept the diagnosis of bipolar, I have had to view life through a different lens. This employer has seen me for my nursing ability also, clearly practising principles surrounding equality and diversity. I couldn't have asked for a better management and nursing team.[12]

Concerning my professional development, I now approach this with caution. I am mindful of what further academic study I commit to. Although I do not want to take

---

[12] My employer is fully aware of the publication and promotion of this book.

on too much in addition to my clinical nursing duties, career development is not out of the question; just not to the detriment of my mental wellbeing.

Trying to work with a mental health condition is not easy. I am tirelessly being told to give myself credit for my efforts. Holding down a job is much harder to do compared with a layperson without such a diagnosis. There was a time when employment in general looked unlikely. Having to make career compromises has had a financial impact. I may not be as rich in monetary value, but bipolar has enriched how I practice as a nurse. Managing to consistently wear my nursing blues for the past five years is a good reason to applaud myself.

Like an AAA Battery: Acceptance

In times of mania, I have been compared to a Duracell battery. I have therefore linked the next three chapters to an **AAA** battery:

Acceptance.

Adaptation.

Accomplishment.

One of the biggest challenges with treating bipolar and mental ill health is accepting the diagnosis and the management plan that comes with it.

Years of being monopolised by poor mental health made me develop bitterness and anger. My journey through bipolar stabilisation has been an expedition. For a time, I could not foresee my recovery moving forward and felt that the road diversions had led me to a dead end. My car was stuck on a roundabout, being unable to find the gap to exit. I felt like the diagnosis and therefore the lengthy journey had stunted growth and personal development. Rather than taking one day at a time, I got overwhelmed with the journey ahead of me. I tended to obsess with results and end goals, drawing unrealistic recovery lines in the sand.

Recovery is down to time, patience and the absence of pressure. Rather than a final destination, recovery continues to be ongoing. A large road closure sign was hit when receiving a mental health diagnosis. Resilience has been built by coping with many crossways, steep hills, detours and unexpected roundabouts. Finally, I no longer live in the fast lane, staying in a lower gear, being more compatible with Guernsey roads!

There are still potholes around, signifying that relapses may arise in the future. I now have suspension, in the form of resilience, to cope with these. Each day, my recovery is approached tentatively, with me concluding that there is strength in my vulnerability.

We service our cars regularly for them to run smoothly. Our bodies are no different. They need continual maintenance. Checking in with my mechanic, (my psychiatrist), reflects self-care for my mode of transport; my mind and body.

Without our flaws, it's important to acknowledge that we would be generic clones. That would create a boring world. Being neurodivergent has enforced my individuality. It is paramount to hold on to what I have gained. Bipolar has provided me with additional layers to my character. Gaining maturity and knowledge from my bipolar experiences has helped me take responsibility for my own brain health. The insight I have gained has come from the significant journey I have had to endure.

It is also worth noting that throughout my expedition, weight has also been gained and battled with. One of my good friends rightly said to me: "Earrings will always fit Anna!" This was a classic line that brought light relief.

There is great truth in what my previous (and award-winning) CPN used to repeatedly tell me: "If you do what you've always done, you get what you have always got." Throughout my twenties, I was going around in circles. I was prone to making the same mistakes.

When I was on my career break, something gave. That unhealthy cycle broke. Stopping doing what I had always done enabled me to reap the rewards; respite and wellness. The pieces of my jigsaw finally interlocked.

Alongside the medical management, including medication and psychotherapy, my lifelong recovery is being aided through acts of autonomous self-management. Putting the bipolar ball back in my court, therefore handing the baton back to me, took time to master. Chemicals and professionals can do so much. Making healthy choices plays a key part in the positive management of a chronic condition.

Such choices can keep symptoms at bay and reduce the likelihood of mood episodes and relapses arising. Bipolar unmanaged can cause significant impairment. However, if the right steps are followed, quality of life can be considerably improved.

Self-management tools

The below list demonstrates acceptance in abundance, as it outlines what I have found to work for me:

- Practising the virtue of patience.
- Becoming an expert on the illness.
- Educating those close to me about bipolar.
- Monitoring my moods and symptoms.
- Being self-aware of my triggers and early warning signs.

- Following healthy routines. For example, eating balanced meals, drinking enough fluids and maintaining good sleep hygiene.
- Nurturing mind, body and soul.
- Using cooking as a form of therapy.
- Mastering the skill of baking traditional Guernsey gâche. (My specialty!)
- Cutting back on caffeine, sugar and alcohol.
- Monitoring stimulation of my environment.
- Exposing self to natural light where possible.
- Having a daily focus and structuring my days.
- Practising mindfulness.
- Exercising in moderation.
- Soaking up 'vitamin sea', by sea swimming all year around. This allows me to reap the benefits of cold-water swimming.
- Scheduling in relaxation.
- Listening to self-help podcasts.
- Accessing helpful bipolar resources.
- Making gratitude lists.
- Surrounding myself with both positive affirmations and people.

- Being still and alone in my headspace.
- Avoiding people-pleasing, putting my wellbeing first. I now regularly converse with myself: "What does Anna need to do?"
- Keeping life stressors to a minimum.
- Working with but not against caregivers and my support network, not seeing seeking help as a weakness.
- Maintaining strong social contact and networks.
- Cutting myself some slack occasionally.
- Keeping most of the above up is vital. When life appears to be normalising, this is when it is easy to become complacent.

Taking on the role of a hypothetical 'bank manager' has enriched my self-management. Amusingly, dealing with finances, historically, has not been my forte. The analogy a family friend shared, treats mind and body like a bank account. The focus is on not going overdrawn.[13] The key principle is to not withdraw more money, which is energy,

---

[13] On 02/05/24, Jacqui Ward granted written permission for her 'bank account' analogy to be mentioned.

than what there is to spend.

For example, if I was struggling with sleep, then I should reduce the level of exertion for that day, keeping me in credit, avoiding a negative balance.

Familiarising myself with self-compassion and self-kindness concepts has helped restore my self-esteem. I disliked who I had become. It is easy for a diagnosis to be taken as a personal fault. Under a pseudonym in 2017, I was invited to write an account of my mental health journey which was published in a book written by local author, Anne Le Tissier: *'The Mirror That Speaks Back.'* The brief was to inspire others by conversing with them about how my bipolar affected my self-esteem, body image and self-worth.

The author, Anne, classed me as one of many phenomenal women who have attempted to overcome adversity.[14] This was my first public contribution to such a conversation. This spurred me on to complete my very own book. Anne has also been instrumental in educating me about book writing.

Like natural disasters, it can take seconds for bipolar

---

[14] On 01/06/24, Anne Le Tissier granted written permission for one of her Christian books, *'The Mirror That Speaks Back'* to be discussed.

relapses to cause much devastation to the individual and others close by. The infrastructure that makes up a person can quickly be demolished. When recovering from an earthquake, the restructuring of buildings can take years.

Mental health recovery is no different. Like buildings, my brain has required new foundations to be laid. The self-management techniques listed in this chapter have been the foundations. Such tools have been used as building blocks to restructure a more balanced 'Anna.'

Acceptance is about taking the diagnosis at face value. Ignoring and running from it has been detrimental. I accept that bipolar will always provide a shadow in my life, but one that lets the sunlight in. Not letting bipolar define me, but allowing it to be a part of me, has been essential in reaching positive mental health.

Differentiating between a natural stress reaction to things, and signs of me becoming unwell, is something I'm working on. Just because a mental health diagnosis has been assigned to me, shouldn't mean that every response of mine is linked to bipolar and mental ill health. I might be having a bad and stressful day, just because. As my recovery is becoming more defined, this is naturally falling into place.

My mental health ordeal has forced me to re-set, re-adjust and re-focus my outlook on life. Valuable lessons have been learnt, allowing me to grow as a person. I appreciate and soak up the simplest of life's pleasures now and hold much gratitude for them.

Knowing how close I came to not being here, has made me appreciate my existence. My journaling has demonstrated that I have been significantly unwell at times, but with great effort, I have learnt to master much more challenging manoeuvres than a three-point turn!

Like an AAA Battery: Adaptation

Although living in the grey is positive, I realise that I am a fair distance from being where I want to be in life. I have had to accept and adapt accordingly. The compromises I have had to make have required me to factor in the comprehensive list of self-management tools outlined in the previous chapter into daily living.

The most significant adjustments centred around reducing nursing hours and moving back home. I also had to cease long-haul solo travel, due to the disruption global time differences can have on my medication regime. Routine in all aspects of life has been key to my success, with me preferring a more structured and organised existence.

Naturally, I find it difficult to not constantly compare myself to friends or siblings. I have yearned to live independently, marry and have a family of my own. There is no blueprint path which every young adult should follow, despite the social expectation for this.

It is easy to feel a failure when life doesn't necessarily map out this way. Being hospitalised throughout my twenties caused me to naturally fall behind in making an independent life for myself. My current frustrations prove how well I am now. I am ready to embark on a life outside of mental illness, which we sometimes never thought I would entertain. The feelings of being static are therefore only natural.

When trying to move forward, I have always been in a quandary of knowing when to tell a prospective partner about my mental health past and how much to share. It has been difficult to know when to be transparent. I have a lot more to offer other than the diagnosis. The focus needs to be on how well it can be managed.

Motherhood has been a topic for discussion. Having a mental health diagnosis naturally adds another dimension to becoming a mum. At the age of thirty-two, I was invited for preconception counselling. Despite not being in any position to become a parent at this time, this meeting provided a platform for discussions surrounding logistics and options.

My psychiatrist and perinatal psychiatric nurse wanted to emphasise that motherhood was not completely out of the question. A lot of planning and precision would be required.

I cannot conceive on the medication that is keeping me so well. It can dramatically affect fertility and cause substantial birth defects. There is also risk surrounding pregnancy, with relapses and post-partum psychosis being a potential possibility. Suffering from a reduction in sleep as a result of having a baby could also trigger me to become unwell.

Weighing up whether having a child is worth the noted risks has to be considered. Social services' involvement and mother and baby units were also honestly spoken about in this initial session. Yet again, I was reminded that bipolar can be life-limiting. Being realistic is essential.

Knowing when to stop and when enough is enough has been another learning curve. Once you have been manic and high, it is hard to feel satisfied with normal things that lift you. Take running for example: I always find it difficult to accept the euphoric feeling it gives me due to previous mania experiences, leaving me wanting more.

I naturally have apprehension around fitness and exercise in general. I am fearful that the buzz it gives me may tip me over into a more manic state of mind. This, therefore, forces me to address exercise with caution.

Do all these adaptations matter? I accept that I have had to make compromises and am not living the life I had in mind. However, I am now soaking up the victory of more than five years of stability. It is a stark comparison to the unwell period that went before. It is surprising how free one can feel from the illness's worst bits even though the label and its limitations are still assigned to me.

My life had to be put on hold for over a decade. Since reaching twenty-nine, I can certainly say I have been living and loving life. Many memories have continued to be made. On my travels, I found this poignant quote nailed to a tree: "Memories are the architecture of our identity." Mum and I have certainly recaptured some of the time lost. Taking up multiple opportunities in a controlled fashion has allowed me to make up for lost time.

I even find pleasure when partaking in simple and mundane tasks, helping to normalise life. Such chores were taken away from me during the countless hospitalisations endured. I am also mindful not to worry about life's trivialities.

On the subject of adaptations, the Coronavirus pandemic has to be mentioned. We were all forced to make sacrifices during this unprecedented global situation, conforming to lockdown rules and regulations. This came at a good time in my recovery journey, as I was able to embrace what was being enforced upon us. I tried not to stress about the things we couldn't change. I relished in the induced stillness that lockdown brought. It encouraged a lifestyle change, moving away from thriving and striving to being content with just being.

Appreciating nature, pursuing my love of photography, building on culinary skills and becoming a bookworm structured my spare time. Lockdown demonstrated how far I had come since 2013.

Anna Bowditch

Like an AAA Battery: Accomplishment

When unwell, it has been easy to catastrophise and think that my mental health consumed my twenties. This is not entirely true. It has been important for me to stop, breathe, take a helicopter view, reflect and identify what I have actually accomplished.

Running the Great South Run, in October 2015, was a huge achievement, raising over two thousand pounds for the charity 'MIND.' Once I returned from the secure unit, I turned to running to shift the weight gained from the aforementioned medication. Completing a Tri-a-Tri, (a mini triathlon), in September 2016 was another athletic accomplishment.

Later in April 2017, it was a relief to fulfil my role as bridesmaid at my triplet brother's wedding. This was amidst a period of hospitalisations. Having not long pressed the pause button on my nursing fob watch, I was conscious of having a Christmas with a difference. In December 2017, volunteering in London with the charity Crisis@Christmas was the most humbling experience. My time working with the homeless brought perspective.

When on my career break during the summer of 2018, once a degree of stability had been established, I embarked on a volunteer project with an English charity, Hospices of Hope. I went out to Romania, to help with the summer camps.

These camps enable children with terminal and life-limiting illnesses to make memories, allowing them to find some respite from their conditions. The very structured routine of this volunteer experience worked for me. It made me disciplined with my medication regime and boosted my confidence and self-esteem. The volunteer team had no preconceived judgments or ideas. My bipolar shadow remained in the background.

Coping with being away from my mental health care team and support network of family and friends, demonstrated that my resilience had gone from strength to strength. In recent years, I have returned to Romania, partaking in more volunteer opportunities. I am fortunate to say that the chief executive officer, (CEO), has become a close friend.

As well as Romania, I undertook volunteer community outreach projects pre-, during and post-diagnosis in Zambia, Nepal and Sri Lanka. This entailed working in aids clinics, orphanages and as part of a building project post-tsunami. Vietnam, Thailand and Peru have also been leisurely visited in times of wellness.

It is clear from this, that I have interjected some normality amongst my unwell periods by making memories that are poignant highlights. When travelling to these places, it was always comforting to notice that when sat in the plane, there is always blue sky above the clouds. My twenties, therefore, haven't all been drenched in mental illness. I have grabbed every window of opportunity. Family and friends see my accomplishments as triumphing over adversity.

I am a proud 'Guern' and am grateful to have been brought up on such a beautiful island. As much as I adore Guernsey, going through the majority of my mental health journey on my home island had its drawbacks. Being cared for in my place of work caused boundaries to be confused.

Having only one hospital had its limitations. Guernsey felt suffocating, too many people knew of my bipolar history. This slowed down my recovery. The feelings of shame, judgement and embarrassment were naturally stronger. It was difficult having no control or voice regarding the level of exposure my mental illness had. This has had a lasting effect on my self-confidence, with further improvement needing to be accomplished surrounding this.

I am aware writing this book exposes myself even further, but it is directly from 'the horse's mouth', and I have chosen to do so when the time has felt right!

After being back in employment for over a year, I completed the mental health first aid course in 2020. This course provided me with the skills to reach into people who may be struggling, without being intrusive. Sometimes, people may not be in the position or in the right head space to reach out. You never know what is going on in someone's life.

Being a champion for mental health is part of my ongoing recovery and redefinition of 'Anna.' My main aim now is to see the positive aspects that the diagnosis has brought me, sharing my experiences to benefit the wider community.

After being reliant on the mental health service for almost ten years, discharge sparked natural anxieties. July

2022 saw me being discharged from CPN contact. Mum and I skipped out of the building on discharge day, marking this momentous day with a special meal. I will always require periodic routine outpatient reviews with my psychiatrist. This is due to remaining on psychiatric medication. Intermittent reviews are no different to an annual car service. I am so grateful for the relationship I now have with my current psychiatrist. The reviews are not too frequent and I feel understood and heard.

Being an outpatient instead of an inpatient is an incentive to stay well. Since discharge, I have crossed paths with CPNs who have previously cared for me. It has been rewarding for them to see for themselves the progress I have made. My local mental health facility no longer feels like my second home.

After gaining four years of stability, in the spring of 2023, I applied for a post that was brought to my attention. The role was within the mental health service, 'expert by experience', a lived experience role. As part of ongoing efforts to improve the mental health service in Guernsey, a steering group was set up following an external review. A mental health strategy was launched.

Me and My Shadow

Someone with mental ill-health experience was required to fulfil this role, sitting alongside psychiatrists, local deputies, operational managers and public health personnel. I was delighted to be successful in my application.

From the establishment of the initial mental health strategy group, subgroups in the structure of different working parties naturally formed.[15] In the spring of 2024, this lived experience role came into its own. By invitation, I began attending the working group meetings associated with trauma-informed care and ACEs, with this concept having already been spoken of in chapter three.

Following on from this, I was also invited to sit on another working party, focusing on the implementation of the community crisis pilot. This is centred on providing 'right care, right people.' There is a long-term intention of providing twenty-four-hour mental health care in the community, particularly in the emergency department at weekends.

In times of crisis, it was ironic that I largely required mental health specialist services on a weekend or a bank

---

[15] On 14/06/24, Public Health Services, (Health and Social Care, HSC), granted written permission for the work of the Mental Health Strategy to be described.

holiday. In addition to good crisis management, there have been times when I did not have the best experiences. These have unfortunately stuck with me. There have been anomalies, blurred care pathways and messy referral processes. It was therefore liberating to sit amongst the heads of departments, listed below, when meeting to discuss this pilot:

- Public health practitioners.
- Operational managers for the emergency department and specialist mental health services.
- Mental health practice development lead nurse.
- Emergency mental health responder.
- Joint emergency control centre, (JESCC).
- Guernsey Police.
- Guernsey Ambulance Service.

Although apprehensive about attending my first meeting, I soon found the courage from within to contribute. The group were extremely encouraging and supportive. We are not there yet, but the fact that we are at this point, putting all our different heads together, discussing real-life scenarios, is an achievement in itself.

Me and My Shadow

This lived experience role is in conjunction with my already established nursing part-time position. I never imagined such a radical role reversal. Actively contributing to service improvement methods has finally enabled me to give something back, turning what was such a negative ordeal into something positive.

Fulfilling this role gives value to what I have been through, now that I can help others. It has allowed me to gain respect from the professionals of those services that once provided care to me in my hour of need.

It is a privilege to be in a position to represent fellow service users by speaking on their behalf. Taking up this role has prompted me to recognise that I have conquered a great deal, coming full circle. I intend to give this role more time once this book is on the shelves!

Another accomplishment and one that I am thankful for, is when I drove through a pothole in the road. I had four years of wellness under my seatbelt. Due to increased work stress and a trip away, my medication and sleep routine became altered, sending me slightly off-piste. My psychiatrist and I viewed this as a positive thing to happen. We adjusted medication, increased reviews and within two months, we collectively caught it.

The successful handling of this was down to seamless teamwork between myself, my psychiatrist and my 'sidecar', Mum. Hitting this pothole, made me realise that even though I am striving to live life in the grey, it is not always going to be so clear-cut. I will naturally pass through the less desirable shades at times.

Life can throw curve balls. At the beginning of 2024, one was thrown my way. Having such high myopia, (short-sightedness), I have unfortunately developed an eye condition, myopic degeneration. Eyes are the windows of our world. Having the future of my sight brought into question has been a lot to digest.

My response to this unexpected diagnosis was in keeping with how other people would perhaps deal with this. I lacked the magnification of an extreme emotional reaction, reiterating how well I am. Having residual strength demonstrates that I have fuel left in my tank to deal with the throwing of the odd-hand grenade!

Although the larger destructive potholes in the road have evened out, as I drive on my life-long road of recovery, I continue to have to face and swerve through further obstacles.

During the summer of 2024, it became very challenging to get hold of my antipsychotic medication on the island. This had a knock-on effect to how I functioned daily, also impacting my working hours as a nurse. Again, my already established resilience stood me in good stead to adapt accordingly for the interim. This demonstrated that I can take these slight deviations in my stride.

I try not to see bipolar and my neurodiverse ways as a weakness. In a clinical review, when I spoke about my shadow in this way, my psychiatrist was very quick to correct me. The stigma I have faced has contributed to this viewpoint of mine. In contrast, friends and work colleagues now use me as an example when helping anyone they know who may be despairing, seeing me as a success story.

When I look back, I feel unrecognisable, almost dissociated from the unwell person that I had become. This is due to the extraordinary recovery I have now made.

To summarise: managing daily life with bipolar and autistic traits, rekindling a solid relationship with my precious 'sidecar', returning to nursing, contributing to mental health service improvement and being in remission of bipolar for just over five years, are my biggest accomplishments to date. Not forgetting writing my memoir!

Navigating the minefield that publishing alone creates has prompted even more resilience to be built!

Roadworthy

You will soon be able to unfasten your seatbelts as you enter this final chapter. Everyone, to some extent, is continuously living and riding on their own rollercoaster of life. I hope to continue to travel through my newfound route without the drastic magnification of the peaks and troughs.

My life since diagnosis, has followed the sequence of a traffic light. It has gone from:

- Red: Causing me to come to an abrupt emergency stop when receiving the bipolar diagnosis.
- Amber: Where I have paused, engaged in self-discovery and fathomed out how to be the best version of myself, with my bipolar shadow and neurodiverse ways.
- Green: Where I have got back in the driver's seat, navigating the new road network diversion, ensuring positive mental health is maintained. This has required me to master the art of using the accelerator and break again, in equal measure.

The work of an 'electrician' has finally been a success!

I am now operating that dimmer switch and reaping the rewards of 'mood lighting!'. The fuse that got blown has been changed. Eventually, I accepted the mental health (Forrest Gump) chocolate that I consumed in my teens, but I have not been so accepting of the world I have had to digest it in.

Ironically, in the next breath, I thank those who did throw obstacles in the way of my recovery. This includes those who crossed the road to avoid speaking and those who no longer speak. I have felt ostracised at times. You have all encouraged me to become more resilient.

Despite how hard it has been, I was not going to be defeated by the stigma that follows a mental health diagnosis. Although I have lost some friends, I have maintained and gained friendships that I treasure to this day. The movement to make mental health more integrated into today's society is gradually improving.

Psychology in the pub sessions is another major step forward when it comes down to awareness. These organised evenings bring common life topics into an informal but sociably acceptable public place. Over a pint, glass of wine or orange juice, mental health conversations arose, attempting to break down that stigma.

Life is now so pressured for school-age children. When I was at school, mental health was the elephant in the room. It has come to light, that mental health is now becoming very much part of the school curriculum. Some schools have even appointed designated mental health support workers and pastoral teams. This is promising progress.

I do perceive that my life's copybook has been blotted due to the mental health diversion I faced. When I consider how right life was going for me before I reached seventeen, I never envisaged what was ahead. Coming back from the documented setbacks and more, indicates the significant recovery I have managed to grasp and sustain.

Reflecting back at the time I found myself standing on a train platform in London Victoria, where police officers and my eldest brother came to the rescue, prompts a feeling of both relief and gratitude for how that situation panned out. It also highlights the breadth of the journey I have been on. I have had to pinch myself. It has been hard to believe all that has happened to me when I am so well now. I am thankful that I haven't yet had an ending.

On several occasions, this could have so easily been a different story, one that I unfortunately would have been unable to have written about.

As briefly mentioned earlier, when contemplating whether to write, I had natural anxieties surrounding the concept of oversharing. My willingness to be brave and therefore vulnerable, by sharing the challenging circumstances encountered, will hopefully have a positive impact on people's understanding, both in the professional and non-professional world.

I have finally forgiven myself for this documented period of mental illness. Forgiveness is not required on second thoughts, as mental ill health is not a personal fault. A period of mental ill health is simply a possibility of life. I am slowly learning to like/love myself again.

Please erase judgements, don't write me off just because of a significant mental health past. My car has been successfully restored. I am roadworthy again!

It has been officially documented that I am now in remission of bipolar. Recovery is not a linear line; it is a wiggly one. Although in remission, I will always be a work in progress. I am now equipped with the skills to deal with any blip adequately.

Better days do come, the downpours cannot last forever. Likewise, road closures have to reopen eventually. They are only temporary, even in Guernsey!

When I was striving for stability, the idea that you can live a successful life with bipolar seemed so out of reach. I doubted having a future. As experienced, a mental health condition can be so catastrophic and damaging when it is not identified in a timely manner, not managed or accepted. Once these elements are addressed, the recovery phase can begin.

My victories have already been discussed, but it is refreshing to look at and celebrate the impressive achievements of famous personnel with bipolar diagnoses. If the condition is managed, there is clearly room for creative and worthy attainments. Bipolar has affected even the most notorious individuals. There are too many to list, but I have picked out a few who have inspired me; Frank Bruno, Stephen Fry and Ruby Wax. Also, the late Vincent Van Gough, Ernest Hemingway and Winston Churchill.

I look at the listed famous individuals and believe there must be a link between the diagnosis of bipolar and creativity and flare. Their accomplishments are all remarkable.

Enduring mental health illness has been lonely and frightening. Inviting you all into my world by publicising my scribblings should have addressed that lonely feeling.

On a trip to Italy in the autumn of 2024, I came across a barrel of olives. I captured this imagery on camera. There were hundreds of black olives, with one lonesome green one in the entire crop. This imagery prompted me to relate it to my mental health. I have often felt like that one green olive; alone and different. However, I have learnt along the way that mental health touches everyone at some point in all of our trajectories of life.

I hope you all have had moments where you have related to me and my 'sidecar's' words. Shouting out: "That's me!", or "That's how I felt!"

Today, there is no reason for us to feel like this one green olive, when you consider the increased awareness and education surrounding mental health that is being projected.

Elements of my journey have also been damaging, causing flashbacks of the worst bits to be experienced from time to time. However, this has just taken time for them to be processed and dealt with.

My story should provide hope for anyone striving for recovery. Being taken off that 'dual carriageway' allowed me to turn my life around. The diagnosis has changed the trajectory of my life. Ordinary stories should resonate and be heard as equally as those shared by famous figures.

As this book closes, the metaphorical language I have used throughout also meets a stop sign! There will not be a sequel, as in my eyes at the age of thirty-six, I am confident that I have conquered the worst bits of this illness. Now that things have fallen into place, I am cruising along the mental health road in an automatic car, confidently test-driving the new me. I have mastered the art of steering again.

Once the right blend of medication and self-help tools were finally established, my fuel gauge went from empty to full in no time.

I will leave you with something that will amuse you. Picture this, days before my thirtieth birthday while collecting my monthly medication supply, my car broke down in the car park outside our local mental health hospital. An auto breakdown vehicle was required. For once, it was refreshing to see that this breakdown was of a different kind;

a real mechanical one! The irony!

Thank you for taking the time to read 'Me and My Shadow.' If you don't have bipolar, I hope this book has enriched your knowledge and understanding about the condition, allowing you to comprehend what it is and more importantly isn't.

For those who do have bipolar, and other mental health conditions for that matter, please remember to stick with it. Shafts of light will peer in and illuminate your shadow. I hope that I have empowered you to believe that it is worth putting the effort in, you have to want to get better and that recovery IS possible.

You can get there, and if you relapse, you can get back. I held so much self-doubt for my recovery along the way, but I got there.

Receiving a mental health diagnosis and weighing up the treatment plans and life's compromises that come with it, can be overwhelming. I can safely say it is worth treating, as my life has been able to be resumed with amendments. I now take great pride and care in maintaining the most precious asset I own; my mind.

Please ignore the myth that a mental health

breakdown can be 'snapped out of.' If it were that easy, I would have, ten years prior! Aged twenty-three, I was forced to stand at a crossroads, not seeming to have a choice about which path to take.

The mental health path was chosen for me, but I have trodden down it successfully and many life lessons have been learnt along the way. The distance I had to travel became a wellness journey, where I overcame many of life's roadblocks.

Victor Hugo's famous words were branded around the island during those Coronavirus lockdown days. They sum up my journey and reinforce that the darkness will always lighten:

"Even the darkest night will end and the sun will rise."
-Victor Hugo, Les Misérables.

Anna Bowditch

"A friend is someone who understands your past, believes in your future, and accepts you just the way you are."

-Anon.[16]

Thank you to all my 'car mechanics', my family and my friends, for getting me back on the road…

---

[16] Quotation by an Anonymous Author. Taken from Bertolucci, D. (2012) *Love Your Life* London: Hardie Grant Books, pp.12. Retrieved November 14, 2024.

Acknowledgements

Main contributors to the book

Special credit goes to:

- Roseanna Courtney: Cover illustration and design. Rosie captured my brief and specifications superbly.

- Jesame Bowditch, (Mumsie): Proofreader extraordinaire. She made an outing out of the tedious task, taking a chapter to a different beach. Days were spent looking over multiple versions of my manuscript. Not to mention her valuable parental contribution in her chapter and for simply being my precious 'sidecar.'

- Tony Brassell: Tony became my self-publishing mentor, always at the end of an email.

- George Russell: George helped with the final technical publishing hurdle.

- Lucy & Luke Vidamour: Lucy was my Microsoft Word wizard and Luke facilitated a vital final edit.

- Jilly Chadwick: Jilly encouraged me to write my story. She polished the pages by patiently editing, also

contributing to book promotion.
- Nick Le Messurier: Nick, my past GCSE English teacher, provided local media contacts.
- Guernsey MIND: They have been instrumental in helping my story become public.
- Anne Le Tissier: Anne gave invaluable book writing advice.

.

Many references to cars and driving in general were made throughout this book. Writing in this style has hopefully made my story more relatable. When unwell and clapped out, I may have hit a wing mirror or two, burnt the clutch and stalled! I have needed all the love and support to be roadworthy again.

I have been lucky enough to have the finest team of mechanics working on me. You know who you are. Family and friends are the best resources we can have. While supporting me, they still had their own lives to lead. If I have missed anyone out, it is unintentional. The focus has been on the support I received during the most turbulent times of my mental health ordeal.

Those encased in the car sketch have given me

strength, helping me to reach the 'there' in the phrase, "You will get there." [17]

My gratitude extends to those who visited me in hospital, listened and encouraged me to persevere. It has not been an easy journey for all involved. Even though I had given up hope at times, you all persisted in being the marshals putting me back on that track.

You have made me realise that I am Anna WITH bipolar and neurodivergent ways, not Anna who IS bipolar. As a result of the fine work carried out by my skilled mechanical team, my bipolar shadow has now progressively and successfully been able to become that desired shade of grey.

In the words of Claudia Winkleman and Tess Daly that famously say: "Keep dancing", I have listened to those of you who have strongly persuaded me to "Keep writing!" This book is therefore the end product of such encouragement.

---

[17] Those listed and those encased within the car illustration have all provided written or verbal permission for their names or descriptions of roles to appear in 'Me and My Shadow.'

Mumsie
DIVERSION
GP PSYCHIATRIC HEALTHCARE PROFESSIONALS
EMPLOYMENT SUPPORT OFFICER
NURSING extended
FRIENDS family
GERALDINE CHELMICK
Julie Lowe
Auntie Joan
THE SUB SISTERS
EMA GIRARD
STEPH REDDALL
LUCY VIDAMOUR
CAROL MOSS
CAITLIN FULLER
Mich Vermeulen
HELEN KIARA Anna
SENSI WALSH Woods
Judith Scott ENID GIRARD
DENISE Angela +
BRETON Bob Abel
Tim, Matt + Georgina Bowditch
JO Laljéeahl
Lisa + Greville Mitchell
nieces + nephews
BECKY OZANNE
LISE FITZSIMMONS
LUCY FLEMING

Disclaimer

'Me and My Shadow' is a memoir based on personal lived experience. The author has done her utmost in anonymising any fellow patients and healthcare professionals met along the way by generalising.

The use of quotations taken from other works has been kept to a minimum, but some powerful quotations have enriched this story. Sourcing information has been footnoted and all authors of the quotations have been clearly documented.

Author Biography

Photograph taken by: Timothy Bowditch, Anna's eldest brother

ANNA BOWDITCH is a first-time author. She has contributed to the mental health conversation due to her unexpected lived experience of mental ill health.

She was born in Southampton in 1988 due to being one of triplets. She lives and works on the beautiful island of Guernsey, which has always been her home. She is known to be a true 'Guern!'

Anna gained a first-class honours degree in nursing back in 2010. Being diagnosed with bipolar at the age of twenty-three caused a disruptive road diversion in Anna's life and career. Nurses get sick too. Despite a pause when striving to reach sustained wellness, Anna has remained in nursing since qualifying on the island and has taken up volunteer opportunities abroad.

She put pen to paper at every stage of her journey, providing a rounded account of what she has endured. It would be her ambition for these scribblings to inspire anyone touched by mental health, allowing Anna to be a mental health champion.

Her empathy, resilience, appetite for life's opportunities and quirky ways, are what her family and friends love most about Anna.

Printed in Great Britain
by Amazon

58704163R00086